THE FEMININE FINANCE CODE

BREAKING MONEY CHAINS AND BUILDING WEALTH WITH STRENGTH,SOUL,AND SELF-WORTH

"Money is a tool, not your worth — use it to build, not to bind."

MINDEXPAND
BOOKS

EVA DENEUX

Published by MindExpand Publishing Ltd Co
Atlanta, Georgia, USA

ISBN (Hardcover): 978-1-968616-40-3
ISBN (Paperback): 978-1-968616-41-0
ISBN (eBook): 978-1-968616-42-7

Cover design by MindExpand Creative
Edited by MindExpand Publishing Editorial Team

Printed in the United States of America

For permissions and inquiries, contact:
info@mindexpandpublishing.com
www.mindexpandpublishing.com

For every woman who's ever carried quiet financial shame — this is your permission to rise.

"There is no limit to what we can become when we stop measuring our worth by what we earn."

– Eva Deneux

Table of Contents

Preface....vii

Introduction....viii

Chapter 1 - Money Is a Tool, Not My Worth....1

Chapter 2 - Basic Training – Budgeting with Purpose....12

Chapter 3 - From Setback to Comeback – Rebuilding Your Finances....17

Chapter 4 - Saving Grace – Building Your Safety Net....23

Chapter 5 - Earn Your Worth – Growing Your Career and Income....30

Chapter 6 - The Side Hustle Sisterhood – Creating New Income Streams....35

Chapter 7 - Failing Forward – My Entrepreneurship Journey....45

Chapter 8 - Money Habits and Daily Hustle – Your Financial Routine....54

Chapter 9 - Credit and Debt – Taming the Two-Headed Monster....64

Chapter 10 - Investing Made Simple – Let Your Money Grow....83

Chapter 11 - The Calm Investor: Building Wealth Without Fear....88

Chapter 12 - Your Financial Freedom Milestones: From Surviving to Thriving....96

Chapter 13 - The Feminine Future: Designing Wealth That Reflects Who You Are....104

Chapter 14 - Legacy of Love – Planning for the Future....110

Epilogue....115

Acknowledgements....120

Continue the Journey....121

Reflection Pages....122

About the Author....125

Preface

Dear Reader,

If I could sit across from you right now – maybe on a quiet couch with a warm drink in hand – I would tell you this: **you are not alone on this journey.** Money is personal. It holds our stories, our fears, our triumphs, and sometimes even our shame. I didn't always understand that. For a long time, I thought money was about status and stuff and getting ahead. I wish someone had told me earlier that money isn't about any of that. It's not about what car you drive or the shoes you wear. And it's definitely not a measure of your worth as a person.

I wrote this book because I know what it's like to lose it all. I also know what it takes to rebuild from the ground up, with faith, support, and some serious grit. This is not your typical finance book. You won't need a business degree or a huge savings account to follow along. Instead, you'll find stories and guidance from someone who's been where you are – confused, overwhelmed, but hopeful that things can change. Think of this book as a conversation with a girlfriend who's been there. I'm going to share the good, the bad, and the ugly of my own money journey, with warmth and without judgment.

So, whether you're just getting started or starting over again, I hope these pages feel like a heart-to-heart chat. We'll talk about faith and finances, about shame and self-worth, about practical tools and big dreams. We'll rewrite some old money stories that have been holding you back and script new ones that empower you. We're in this together. And this time, **we're writing our own code.**

With love,
Eva

Introduction

At 22 years old, I thought I had it made. I had just purchased my first house – a milestone that felt like the pinnacle of the American Dream for a young woman like me. As an immigrant from Sierra Leone who came to America as a child, owning a home at 22 made me feel unstoppable. I was in the U.S. Air Force, earning a steady paycheck, and accumulating the kind of material success my parents could only have dreamed of. From the outside, it looked like I was winning at this money game.

Then I lost everything. A few short years later, that house was gone (along with my savings), and I found myself starting over from scratch. How did that happen? In hindsight, the warning signs were there all along – I had been learning about making money and accumulating things, but I hadn't yet learned how to manage money or, more importantly, the mindset behind it. I hadn't unlearned the shaky financial habits and beliefs I'd grown up with. In other words, I was building a house on no foundation, and eventually it collapsed like a house of cards. I had to face a tough truth: having money isn't the same as understanding money.

Let me back up a bit and introduce myself. I'm Eva Deneux, and my story is probably a lot like many others – full of ups and downs, mistakes and comebacks. I moved to America at a young age to join my parents who were already here. My parents, both immigrants, came from a world with very different financial norms. In Sierra Leone, they didn't use credit cards, invest in stocks, or navigate complex bank systems. They believed in working hard and saving what you earned in cash. If you couldn't afford it, you simply didn't buy it. As a result, I inherited some of those beliefs. We never talked about credit scores or 401(k)s at home. In fact, everything from opening a bank account to filing taxes and saving for retirement felt foreign to my family. We weren't unintelligent – my parents are some of the smartest people I know – but the American financial system was a whole new world for us, filled with concepts and rules that didn't exist in the country we came from. It's a common hurdle for many first-generation immigrants: Immigrants and first-generation Americans face many barriers to financial literacy, from language hurdles to unfamiliar cultural norms. We certainly did.

Growing up, I absorbed my father's cautious attitude toward money and my mother's more carefree spending habits. "Debt is bad. Banks can't be trusted. Investing is for the rich." These weren't things my parents said outright, but they were underlying beliefs in our household. I now know we weren't alone – many people from other cultures feel the same. With that mindset, I entered adulthood great at scrimping and saving, but with zero experience in building credit or investing for the future. By the time I was in college, I was the friend who kept cash hidden in an envelope because I didn't quite trust banks. I avoided credit cards entirely (because I'd heard horror stories of debt) and thought I was doing well financially if I simply had more money coming in than going out.

After two years in college, feeling restless and eager for independence, I joined the U.S. Air Force. Talk about a crash course in real life! Suddenly I was living on my own salary, surrounded by people from all walks of life – and money was a frequent topic of conversation. I met peers who casually talked about credit scores and car loans, who taught me that not all debt is bad (news to me!), and mentors who urged me to invest in the Thrift Savings Plan (the military's retirement program) even in my early 20s. My world was getting bigger, and I was picking up financial tips here and there, slowly chipping away at the ignorance I didn't even realize I had. With newfound confidence, I took what felt like a very grown-up step: I used my savings and VA loan benefits to buy my first home at 22.

For a while, it seemed like I was on the fast track. Here I was, a 22-year-old homeowner with a steady military job – far ahead of where my parents had been at my age. But underneath that apparent success, I still had the same old money mindset I'd grown up with. Sure, I owned a house, but I didn't have a plan for budgeting beyond paying the mortgage, and I wasn't prepared for life's curveballs. I continued some of the "bad money habits" I'd learned unconsciously: not planning for emergencies, splurging when I felt flush and then panicking when bills came, and avoiding the hard conversations about money. In truth, I was winging it and hoping for the best. You can guess what happened next – life humbled me. A few poor decisions and a couple of financial setbacks later, I was in over my head. I fell off the financial wagon – hard. Ultimately, I lost that home and found myself right back where I'd started, with no property and an almost empty bank account. It was a scary and painful place to be.

Losing everything I'd worked for felt devastating, but in hindsight, it was the wake-up call I needed. Hitting rock bottom forced me to take a brutally honest look at my habits and beliefs. I realized that earning money wasn't my issue – it was keeping it and growing it that I needed to learn. I had to unlearn the scarcity mindset that told me to just clutch tightly to cash and never take calculated risks. I had to confront the fact that I treated money as something that happened to *me* instead of something I could proactively manage. This period of my life was tough, but it set the stage for a transformation. As the saying goes, every setback is a setup for a comeback. I was determined to come back stronger and wiser.

My turnaround began in the unlikeliest of ways. While still in the Air Force, I was unexpectedly assigned to fill in as a budget analyst for a unit on base. It wasn't a role I had asked for – in fact, it was dropped in my lap because they were short-staffed and someone noticed I had a knack for numbers. Suddenly I was responsible for helping manage and report on a high-performing budget (we're talking millions of dollars of Uncle Sam's money). Talk about pressure! But a funny thing happened: I fell in love with budgeting. Yes, the former avoider-of-budgets (me) became utterly fascinated by the process of telling each dollar where to go. In that job, I saw how a plan for your money could make or break an entire operation. I learned to create spreadsheets, forecast expenses, and squeeze savings out of even the tightest ledgers. It clicked for me that if I could manage the Air Force's money, I could darn well manage my own. I started applying those skills to my personal life, tracking my spending and setting up my first real emergency fund. It felt empowering to finally be in control of my money rather than the other way around.

That spark led me to go back to school after my military service. I earned a degree in accounting and later a master's in accounting and finance. I was hungry to deepen my knowledge and truly understand the mechanics of personal finance and business. Each stage of my education and career pulled back another curtain on the world of money. I learned *why* credit scores matter (and how to improve them), the rationale behind investing in stocks and bonds, and the psychology of financial decision-making. Perhaps most importantly, I started recognizing the mindset piece of the puzzle – how our beliefs and attitudes toward money impact the results we get. I saw it in myself, and I saw it in others.

After graduate school, I embarked on a new career as a stockbroker and financial advisor. Talk about a front-row seat to people's finances! In that role, I worked with families and individuals from all walks of life. I saw clients who, despite having good incomes, struggled because of poor habits or fear-based decisions. I also saw modest earners build substantial wealth through discipline and planning. This confirmed something huge for me: financial success is as much about mindset and behavior as it is about math. Knowing what to do isn't enough; you have to actually *do* it, and that takes the right mindset.

Each chapter of my journey – from the careless young airman with a maxed-out credit card, to the budget officer finding joy in spreadsheets, to the stockbroker guiding clients through market ups and downs – revealed a new lesson about money *and* about myself. I've made every mistake in the book (and wrote this book so you don't have to!). I also turned many of those mistakes into wins, once I learned how. Along the way, I transitioned from that penny-pinching, risk-averse girl into a woman who is confident about her finances and excited about her future.

That's why I wrote this book. I want to take everything I've learned – through formal education, professional experience, and plenty of real-life trial and error – and share it with you in these pages. Think of this book as our candid conversation over coffee. I'll be sharing my personal stories (the good, the bad, and the cringe-worthy) and the exact strategies that helped me transform my finances and mindset. We'll talk about faith and finances, shame and self-worth, practical tools and big dreams.

Here's what you can expect as we journey together through these chapters:

–**Chapter 1: Money Is a Tool, Not My Worth**

–**Chapter 2: Budgeting with Purpose**

–**Chapter 3: From Setback to Comeback**

–**Chapter 4: Saving Grace**

–**Chapter 5: Earn Your Worth**

–**Chapter 6: The Side Hustle Sisterhood**

–**Chapter 7: Failing Forward**

–**Chapter 8: Money Habits That Stick**

–**Chapter 9: Credit and Debt Made Simple**

–**Chapter 10: Investing Made Simple**

–**Chapter 11: The Calm Investor**

–**Chapter 12: Your Financial Freedom Milestones**

–**Chapter 13: The Feminine Future**

–**Chapter 14: Legacy of Love**

This isn't just a finance book – it's a faith-filled guide to rebuilding your confidence, rewriting your money story, and reclaiming your power. By the end, I hope you'll see that financial freedom isn't about perfection or privilege – it's about peace, purpose, and persistence.

So grab your favorite drink, settle in, and let's begin this journey toward financial empowerment together. You don't need to have it all figured out; you just need to take the first step.

Chapter 1

Money Is a Tool, Not My Worth

Tiny Rituals That Rewired Me: *(Little habits can spark big changes. Here are two small rituals that helped change my money mindset early on.)*

- **Pause Before You Swipe:** I put a tiny sticky note on my debit card that asks, *"Do you really need this, or do you just need a breath?"* This gentle pause makes me stop and reflect before spending impulsively. It has saved me more times than I can count by interrupting the emotional impulse to buy and giving me a moment to choose differently.
- **Voice Notes to Myself:** Whenever I feel scared to ask for a raise, to say no to an expense I can't afford, or to hit "submit" on a tough financial decision, I record a quick voice note on my phone. In it, I whisper the encouragement I need to hear, something like, *"You're not that panicked girl at the register anymore. You've got this."* Later, I play it back. Hearing my own voice speaking courage and truth over my fears is surprisingly powerful and comforting.

Now, let's begin our journey. I'll start by sharing my story – with all its twists and turns – and together we'll unpack the lessons, tools, and truths that form the **Feminine Finance Code**. Ready to get started? Turn the page, grab life by the budget (yes, I said it!), and let's walk this path toward financial empowerment **together**.

Let's do this, together.

From Cash Culture to Foreclosure

I grew up in Sierra Leone, a place where cash was king. In my childhood community, almost no one had a bank account – as recently as a few years ago, about 80% of Sierra Leoneans were "unbanked." Money was literally paper and coins changing hands for rice, for school fees, for doctor visits. I learned early that money could buy things we needed, but it wasn't some abstract number on a screen, and it certainly wasn't a measure of a person's value. Money was neutral – useful and necessary, yes, but never the definition of a person.

But there was something deeper happening beneath the surface, even if I did not have the language for it at the time. Sierra Leone shaped my understanding of money not just on a practical level but on an emotional one. In my community, people shared what they had, stretched what seemed impossible, and held one another up when times were hard. Wealth was not defined by bank accounts or investments. It was defined by generosity, responsibility, and how well you cared for your family and the people around you. The way I saw women manage money was especially formative. Women stretched small amounts with creativity and intention. They made a little feel like a lot. That quiet strength became part of my foundation.

Fast forward a decade. At 22 years old, I was serving in the U.S. Air Force and I proudly owned my first home. Buying that house so young made me feel accomplished. I thought I was "ahead" in life, checking off the American Dream.

That pride came crashing down when an unexpected financial storm hit. I lost the house to foreclosure, and along with it, I felt like I lost my identity. I will never forget watching the padlock go on the front door. I was overwhelmed with shame, thinking, *"If I can't even keep my own house, what does that say about me?"*

In that moment, my net worth felt exactly like my self-worth. But this is where my early money conditioning from Sierra Leone came back to me in ways I did not expect. I grew up surrounded by people who faced real hardship with strength, and those images shaped the way I understood resilience. My immediate family had stability, but the community around us was filled with stories of making do, rebuilding, and supporting one another in ways that went far beyond financial circumstances.

What influenced me most, though, was watching my grandmother. She only birthed two children, yet she raised more than seventy. She paid school fees for children whose parents could not, opened her home to anyone who needed care, and carried her heart for service across borders in her work with the United Nations. She was known not just in our community but across Sierra Leone and even in other countries for her belief that every child deserved a chance. Watching her created a blueprint for me long before I knew the word "financial literacy." She taught me that money is only powerful when it is used with intention, compassion, and responsibility. She showed me that provision is not about abundance, but about willingness.

Remembering her softened the blow. I had seen resilience in action my entire life. I had seen people lose far more than a house and still rise again. I had seen children given futures because one woman believed they were worth investing in. Those memories reminded me that while I was hurting, I was not ruined. The same strength I witnessed growing up whispered to me in that dark moment, even when I could barely hear it.

In my lowest moment, I found myself whispering a new mantra: *"Money is a tool, not my worth."* I repeated it to myself like a lifeline. Little by little, it sank in. **Money, at its core, is neutral – it's a tool for exchange and survival, not a definition of who you are.** Losing the house hurt, yes, but it didn't make me a bad person or a failure as a human being. It simply meant my financial toolset needed some work. This realization lifted a huge weight off my shoulders.

I want to hand that same freedom to you, right here and now. Whatever your financial situation or mistakes, you have **permission to drop the shame.** Your bank balance is not a report card on your character. Your worth is beyond any dollar amount. It doesn't matter if you're drowning in debt, living paycheck to paycheck, or sitting on a savings cushion – money does **not** determine your value. You are worthy of respect and love regardless of your financial status.

Let's reframe money for what it really is: a useful tool we can learn to handle, **not** a mirror reflecting our self-esteem.

The Money Messages We Inherit

If you think about it, many of our beliefs about money didn't originate with us. We all inherit *"money messages"* from various sources while growing up – our families, our culture or faith, even the media. These early messages quietly shape how we feel about earning, spending, and what we believe we deserve. Psychologists even have a term for these ingrained beliefs: **"money scripts"**, meaning the unconscious stories about money we pick up as children and carry into adulthood. Let's look at a few common sources of these money messages:

- **Family:** Our parents and relatives are our first money teachers. Perhaps you heard things like *"We can't afford that"* or *"Money doesn't grow on trees."* Hearing those repeatedly might have planted the idea that money is always scarce, or that wanting things is selfish. On the other hand, maybe money was a taboo topic in your house – polite families just didn't talk about it at all. The attitudes you saw at home – whether it was extreme frugality, constant anxiety about bills, or free-spirited spending – often stick with you for life. We tend to either emulate our family's approach or react against it, but either way, those early lessons run **deep**.
- **Faith and Culture:** Your spiritual and cultural background might send mixed signals about money. Some religious teachings warn that *"money is the root of all evil"* or praise the virtues of poverty, which can make you feel guilty for having or even wanting money. Other faiths or cultures might see financial success as a sign of God's blessing. If you grew up hearing that wealth is sinful *or*, conversely, that prosperity equals virtue, it's no wonder you might feel confused or conflicted about money. These beliefs can lead to guilt, shame, or an internal tug-of-war over whether it's okay to seek financial success.

- **Media and Society:** From TV shows to Instagram feeds, we're bombarded with the idea that success equals having lots of money and shiny things. Society often equates self-worth with net worth, sending the subtle message that if you're not rich, you're not as valuable. Think about the last movie or ad you saw that featured a "successful" person – chances are, they had the big house, the luxury car, the designer clothes. These media images can make us subconsciously measure ourselves against a money yardstick. If you've ever felt "behind" because your life doesn't look like those glossy magazine spreads, you've absorbed the message that more money = more worth. It's a false and toxic narrative, but a powerful one that many of us internalize before we even realize it.

Now, none of these money messages are inherently true. They are scripts written by others – family attitudes, cultural teachings, marketing tactics – not by you. Yet they run in the background of our minds and influence our choices. For example, there's a common money script called "money status," where people define their self-worth by their net worth. If you've ever felt like earning a higher salary made you a "better" or more capable person, or that a low bank balance made you a failure, that's money-status thinking at work. **Recognizing** these inherited beliefs is the first step. You can't change a script you haven't identified. So ask yourself: **What money messages did I grow up with? Which of them have I unwittingly accepted as truth?**

The Deeper Layer of Your Money Story

Now that we have explored where money messages come from on the surface, it is time to peel back the next layer. Every woman carries a money story. It does not begin when you get your first job or open your first bank account. It begins in childhood, long before you know what money really is.

Your money story is shaped by small moments you may not remember clearly but that left emotional footprints. Maybe you watched adults argue about bills. Maybe you saw a caregiver stretch meals in ways that taught you scarcity without anyone ever saying the word. Maybe you felt pride when you had your own small earnings as a child. Maybe you were told not to ask for too much. Maybe money was used to show love. Maybe it was used to control. Maybe it was in short supply. Maybe it flowed freely. All of those experiences formed the invisible framework you stand on today.

The emotions tied to these early experiences matter. They shape how you respond to financial stress, how you make decisions, and how you feel about what you deserve. You may not remember the details, but your reactions remember.

Let me share a few examples that illustrate how deeply childhood conditioning carries into adulthood.

One woman kept buying cheap, uncomfortable shoes even though she could afford better ones. She eventually realized she had inherited her mother's belief that spending money on herself was wasteful. Her behavior made perfect sense once she understood her story.

Another woman felt a rush of shame every time her business made a profit. She traced it back to being scolded as a child for keeping leftover change after running an errand. The message she absorbed was that wanting money was wrong.

A third woman refused to invest no matter how much advice she received. Her fear came from watching her father lose his job. The emotional imprint told her that money could vanish without warning, so she clung to every dollar for safety.

And another woman struggled to negotiate her salary because she grew up hearing that "good girls don't make demands." Even as a successful professional, she hesitated to advocate for herself because the childhood script had taught her that asking was a form of disrespect.

These stories are not flaws. They are insights. They explain why you react the way you do, and once you understand the story behind the behavior, you gain the power to choose differently.

Real Talk:

You cannot rewrite your money habits until you understand who handed you the pen.

Recognizing your money story is not about blaming your past. It is about understanding it so you can move forward with clarity, compassion, and choice. Awareness opens the door. Choice is what lets you step through it.

Where Your Story Came From

Your money story is a blend of:

- The environment you grew up in
- The emotions tied to early money moments
- The messages spoken and unspoken
- The fears and hopes of the adults around you
- The survival strategies your community relied on

You did not choose these beliefs. But you get to choose what happens next.

Awareness gives you power.
Compassion gives you clarity.
Choice gives you freedom.

When Net Worth ≠ Self-Worth (Especially for Women)

Everyone can struggle with tying their identity to money, but women in particular face unique pressures in this arena. Culturally, women have long been dealt a double financial burden: social expectations on one side and systemic inequalities on the other. The result is that many women subconsciously internalize the idea that if their finances aren't in perfect order, *they themselves* are "not good enough." Let's unpack a few reasons behind this:

- **The Wage Gap:** Even today, there is a persistent income disparity between men and women. On average, women earn about 82 cents for every dollar a man earns – and Black and Latina women earn even less. Over a lifetime, that wage gap adds up to a massive difference in wealth and financial security. Imagine working just as hard as someone else but effectively being told your work – *you* – are valued 18% less. It's not hard to see how that can chip away at one's sense of worth. When society literally pays you less for the same effort, the insidious message is that you are worth less. This is absolutely not true on a human level, but the financial facts can make it *feel* true emotionally.

- **The "Pink Tax" & Financial Double Standards:** As if earning less isn't bad enough, women are often charged more for the very same things. The *"pink tax"* refers to the markup on products marketed to women – studies show women's products cost about 7% more on average than similar products for men. Everything from razors to shampoo to clothes often costs more when it's pink or "for her." We're essentially penalized for being female consumers. Beyond products, consider how women are expected to maintain a certain appearance – cosmetics, hair, clothing – which often means spending more money just to meet basic professional or social standards. All of this can lead to frustration and a sense of unfairness that, again, can sneakily erode how a woman values herself. It's easy to subconsciously think, *"I have less savings or higher expenses; why can't I manage better?"* without realizing the playing field is tilted against you from the start.
- **Social Scripts and Shame:** From a young age, many girls receive subtle (or not-so-subtle) social scripts about money: *"Men are better with money." "A woman's role is to be nurturing, not negotiating." "Talking about money is unladylike."* While these stereotypes are outdated, they still linger in media tropes and in advice from older generations. If you've ever felt hesitant to ask for a raise, or found yourself letting your partner handle investments because you've been told "he's the numbers guy," you've felt the pull of these scripts. They can breed a sense of insecurity around money management (*"I'm just not good with money, so my financial mess is my own fault"*) or cause you to tie your worth to roles like being a good mother or caregiver at the expense of your financial growth. Women also often carry the expectation to "do it all" – have a successful career **and** be the primary

caregiver at home **and** look effortlessly put-together. It's an impossible bind. When any piece slips (say you scale back work to care for a child and your income drops), it's easy to let self-criticism creep in: *"I'm failing, I'm not enough."*

It's important to shine a light on these external pressures, because the problem isn't you – it's the unfair environment and narratives that have been pushed onto you. If you are a woman reading this and you've ever felt ashamed for not earning more... or guilty for earning more than a partner... or embarrassed about your debt – **know that you are far from alone.** In fact, nearly half of people (women and men alike) feel ashamed about their finances. Money shame is extremely common, and it **thrives in silence.** By acknowledging the societal factors at play, you can start separating your intrinsic worth from the numbers in your bank account.

Now that we've unpacked these toxic messages and pressures, let's start rewriting them. The rest of this chapter is about reclaiming your self-worth from money's grip. We're going to gently untangle those two concepts (your worth vs. your money situation) so you can move forward with confidence and self-compassion.

Rewriting Your Money Story (Exercise)

It's time to challenge the old narratives and replace them with truth. Here are a few steps to help you heal your relationship between money and worth:

1. **Uncover Your Script – Journal It Out:** Take a moment to write down the messages you've believed about money and self-worth. Be honest and compassionate with yourself. What phrases or attitudes come up? ("I can't get ahead," "I'm just bad with money," "Having debt makes me a failure," etc.) Writing these down brings them out of the shadows. Sometimes seeing the words on paper helps you realize how hard you've been on yourself. This is your old money story. Acknowledging it is powerful.
2. **Create a New Mantra (and Feel Free to Steal Mine):** Now that you've identified the old narrative, define a new one. What core belief

do you want to adopt about money and self-worth going forward? It might be as simple as the mantra I used – *"Money is a tool, not my worth."* Or it could be another phrase that resonates with you, such as *"I deserve financial stability,"* or *"I am worthy of happiness whether or not I have money right now."* Keep it short, positive, and present tense (state it like it's already true). If you're struggling, borrow my mantra or one of these: *"I am not my debt." "I am building wealth and worth from the inside out." "Money is my servant, not my master."* The exact words don't matter as much as how they make you feel. You should feel a sense of **relief, empowerment, or peace** when you say them. This mantra is your new lens – use it to replace that old, critical tape running in your mind.

3. **Mirror Exercise – Speak It Aloud:** This one might feel a little silly at first, but trust me, it works. Go to a private spot with a mirror (your bathroom or bedroom works great) and say your new mantra out loud to your own reflection. Look yourself in the eyes and speak it like you're encouraging your dearest friend: *"Money is a tool, not my worth."* Do it today. Then do it again tomorrow, and the day after. Make it a daily ritual for at least the next week. Notice how it feels each time. The first time might be awkward or even emotional – you might hear an inner skeptic or feel a lump in your throat. That's okay. By the third or fourth time, notice if that voice of doubt is getting quieter, and if a hint of confidence is taking its place. Repetition is key. You're effectively **retraining your brain**, building a new mental pathway that links money with neutrality and self-worth with who you are inside. Over time, this simple mirror exercise helps carve a new default belief: *"I am worthy, full stop – and money is just a tool I can learn to use."*

4. **Celebrate Small Wins:** *(Consider this a bonus step to carry forward.)* One of the best antidotes to money shame is actively acknowledging any and all positive steps you take. Did you read a chapter of a personal finance book? High-five! Did you confront a bill you dreaded and set up a payment plan? Fantastic! Did you resist comparing your

paycheck to someone else's and focus on your own goals instead? That's huge. Treat these like the victories they are. Write them down, tell a supportive friend, or literally give yourself a pat on the back. Positive reinforcement isn't childish; it's how we train our brains to keep doing the good stuff. Every time you celebrate a small win, you reinforce the truth that financial progress is about **growth and learning**, not about your worthiness.

Finally, as you work through these steps, be patient and kind to yourself. Unlearning years (or decades) of money shame and fear doesn't happen overnight. There may be days you slip back into old thought patterns – that's normal. When that happens, don't despair. Recognize it as an old tape playing, and consciously hit "pause." Take out your journal, look in the mirror, repeat your mantra – do whatever helps you remember who you **truly** are.

You are not your paycheck. You are not your debt. You are not your credit score. **You are a whole, worthy, capable person who is learning to use money as a tool to build the life you want.** That's it. That's the truth. Whenever you doubt it, come back to this chapter, come back to your own words in your journal, and come back to that person in the mirror. She's amazing, and no dollar amount could ever measure her worth.

Chapter 2

Basic Training – Budgeting with Purpose

After three years of being in the Air Force, an unexpected assignment completely changed my relationship with money. I was suddenly appointed as a squadron budget analyst, tasked with managing millions of Uncle Sam's dollars. Talk about intimidating! I remember staring at spreadsheets of government funds with sweaty palms and a pit in my stomach. I was terrified – I'd never thought of myself as a "numbers girl," and now I was responsible for huge sums. But as the weeks passed, that terror turned into competence, and then (to my own surprise) into *joy*. I learned how to give every dollar a job, allocating funds so precisely that nothing was wasted. It was like solving a giant puzzle every day – and you know what? I actually started having fun with it. If I could manage the military's budget, surely I could manage my own. That unexpected assignment became my personal finance boot camp. It taught me a powerful lesson: **budgeting wasn't a punishment – it could actually be empowering.**

Back then, I had been the type to avoid looking at my bank account until I *had* to. (I used to log in with one eye closed, bracing for bad news at the end of each month.) My finances felt like a mystery novel where I was always dreading the final chapter. But after my "budget boot camp" experience, I decided to try something new. One Friday night, I poured a glass of wine, opened up a spreadsheet, and had my first real **"money date"** with myself. I lit a candle, turned on a chill playlist, and reviewed where my money had been going. Shockingly, it actually felt... fun – or at least not awful! I realized I could make budgeting feel like self-care: a cozy night in dedicated to my future well-being. Instead of punishing myself for past spending, I was caring for my future self. That simple change in mindset (and maybe the wine) turned budgeting from a dreaded chore into something almost enjoyable.

By the end of that evening, I felt calm and in control rather than anxious. The next morning, I wasn't hungover with regret (financial or otherwise); I was excited, because I had a plan for my money. This was a far cry from my old routine. In the past, payday meant **"treat yourself"** time – I'd splurge on takeout, new shoes, little luxuries, as if the cash were burning a hole in my pocket. Within a week or two, I'd be scrounging, wondering *"Where did it all go?!"* Now, with a budget in place, there were no more nasty surprises. I could still treat myself, but in a balanced way that I decided *on purpose.* Budgeting transformed my end-of-month anxiety into confidence and even pride.

Find Your Budgeting Style – Choose Your Weapon

At this point you might be thinking, *"Okay, good for you... but how do I actually budget in a way that doesn't make me miserable?"* Great question! The truth is, budgeting isn't one-size-fits-all. The best budgeting method is one that fits your lifestyle and personality. Let's break down a few popular budgeting styles – consider these your budgeting "weapons" and pick the one that feels right for you:

- **Zero-Based Budgeting:** This method has you allocate every dollar of income to a specific purpose until you have zero dollars left unassigned. In other words, *give every dollar a job* – whether it's paying bills, buying groceries, knocking down debt, building savings, or even fun money, make sure each dollar is accounted for so nothing slips through the cracks. Zero-based budgeting offers great control because you **account for each dollar.** It's what I learned in my Air Force days. (YNAB – short for *"You Need A Budget"* – is a popular app that uses this approach, preaching "give every dollar a job.") **Upside:** you know exactly where your money is going. **Downside:** it can be a bit more work to track everything regularly.

- **50/30/20 Rule:** This is a simple formula for folks who don't want to micromanage every cent. The rule, popularized by Senator Elizabeth Warren and her daughter in their book *All Your Worth,* suggests devoting 50% of your take-home income to needs, 30% to wants, and 20% to savings or debt repayment. For example, if you bring home $4,000 a month, about $2,000 goes to must-haves (rent, utilities, food), $1,200 to "fun" or discretionary spending (dining out, shopping, hobbies), and $800 to your financial goals (building an emergency fund, paying off loans, etc.). This rule is straightforward and ensures you're balancing necessities with some fun and some future security. It's a great starting point if you want a high-level plan without digging into dozens of detailed budget categories.
- **Envelope System:** This is an old-school method that's stood the test of time (and has modern app versions now). The idea is simple: you allocate cash for different spending categories into envelopes each month (or each paycheck). For example, you might have envelopes (literal or digital) for Groceries, Transportation, Eating Out, etc. Once an envelope is empty, that's it – you've hit your limit for that category until next period. This method is **fantastic for overspenders** or anyone who feels out of control with swipe transactions, because it forces you to physically see and limit what you spend in each area. It makes budgeting very tangible. However, dealing with cash can be inconvenient, and if you mostly spend online or by card, you'd use a digital version of this. The envelope system instills discipline by design.
- **"Pay Yourself First" Budgeting:** This approach flips the script by prioritizing saving and investing *before* other expenses. Here's how it works: you decide on an amount or percentage to save from each paycheck (say 10% or a fixed $200), and you automatically transfer that to savings or investments when you get paid. The remaining money is what you use for bills and spending. In essence, you treat savings like

the first bill you must pay. This method is great if building up savings (or paying off debt) is a big goal and you struggle to find money for it after paying all your other bills. By paying yourself first, you make sure your goals are funded, and you live on what's left. It requires a bit of discipline to not dip into the savings later, but automation helps remove temptation.

Whatever method you choose, remember that *your budget is a living thing.* It can be adjusted. The key is to **find a style that you can stick with,** because consistency matters more than perfection. Some people even blend methods – for instance, using the 50/30/20 guideline but also doing zero-based planning for certain categories like groceries. Do what feels comfortable and sustainable for you.

Make Budgeting Yours (Tips & Tricks)

- **Budgeting Dates:** Treat budgeting as a date with yourself. Set aside a specific time each week or month for a "money date" like I did. Light a candle, grab a cup of tea or glass of wine, play your favorite music. Make it something you *look forward to* – a time to care for yourself financially.
- **Name Your Accounts:** Many banking apps let you give nicknames to your accounts. Try renaming your savings accounts to things like *"Italy Trip Fund"* or *"Future Home Down Payment"* or *"Emergency Peace of Mind."* Giving your money a purpose (and a fun name) can motivate you to stick to your plan because you see exactly what you're building toward.
- **Use Tools That Work for You:** If you love pen and paper, get a cute budgeting planner or notebook. If you're a tech person, explore budgeting apps (Mint, YNAB, EveryDollar, etc.) or even a simple spreadsheet. There's no "right" tool – the right one is whatever you'll actually use regularly.
- **Give Yourself Grace:** Some months you'll overspend in a category. Life happens! Instead of seeing it as a failure, view it as feedback.

Adjust your budget for next month and keep going. The goal is progress, not perfection.

Before we wrap up, let's address one of the biggest money myths out there — that budgeting equals deprivation. In truth, budgeting isn't about restriction; it's about freedom. It's not meant to trap you but to empower you. A good budget tells your money where to go so it can serve your dreams instead of disappearing without purpose. When you know your numbers, you gain choice, and choice is freedom. Budgeting gives you control over your priorities, not punishment for spending. Once you start to see budgeting as self-care for your future self, the entire process feels lighter, more intentional, and far more rewarding.

Reflection: Budgeting with Purpose

Take a moment now to solidify your commitment to budgeting with purpose:

Reflect: What's one small expense you can trim this week without much heartache, and what's one budget category you want to give more love to? (For example: maybe cutting one takeout meal and directing $30 to your "dream vacation" savings.)

Write down your answer. This helps connect your budget to your *real life* priorities – less spending on what doesn't matter, more for what does.

Congratulations on taking these first budgeting steps! You've turned budgeting from something scary into something purposeful and even personal. By doing so, you're proving to yourself that **you** control your money – not the other way around. This foundational skill will serve you enormously as we move forward. In fact, it's going to be a lifesaver when life throws curveballs (and it will). But now you'll be ready – with your budget as your armor – to handle setbacks and come out stronger. *(Spoiler alert: in the next chapter, we'll tackle exactly that – how to rebound when things go wrong. But look at you, you've already got some tools in place!)* For now, relish the confidence that comes with having a plan for your money. Your budget is essentially **self-care on paper** – it's you taking care of your own needs and dreams. Keep it up, and trust me, your future self will thank you profusely.

Chapter 3

From Setback to Comeback – Rebuilding Your Finances

Core Purpose: No matter how dire things seem, you can reclaim control of your money and your mindset after a financial setback. This chapter is about triaging a financial mess without spiraling into self-loathing. We're going to learn how to pick up the pieces of a financial disaster with compassion, turning shame and fear into confidence and action.

Hitting Rock Bottom: The Day Everything Collapsed

I'll never forget the day I opened an envelope from the bank and felt my stomach drop. It was a foreclosure notice on my home – official confirmation that I was about to "lose it all." In that moment, a mix of shame, panic, and grief washed over me. I sat on the floor clutching that letter, hot tears streaming down my face. My mind raced: *How did I let it get this bad?* I sat on that floor for what felt like hours, in shock. Then the phone rang. It was the bank's representative politely explaining what came next. My hands trembled as reality set in. It felt like the darkest, most helpless moment of my life.

I cried until there were no tears left. Then came anger – anger at myself for the mistakes that led here, and even anger at the world for throwing me curveballs I hadn't been prepared to catch. If you've experienced a financial catastrophe like this, know that such emotions are normal. Give yourself permission to feel the tears, the rage, even the eventual relief that can come weirdly enough from hitting bottom (sometimes there's a grim calm in knowing *"well, nowhere to go but up now"*). You're not **"weak"** for breaking down; you're human. Feeling the pain is necessary, but *wallowing* in self-pity forever won't help you rebuild. I knew I couldn't stay in that dark pit forever.

Regrouping with Emotional First Aid

After the initial shock, I realized my first priority wasn't a financial tactic at all – it was **emotional first aid.** I had to forgive myself for the missteps that led here and let go of the crippling guilt. Beating myself up wasn't going to pay a single bill; it would only sap the energy I desperately needed to climb out of this hole. So I took a deep breath and literally said out loud: *"I made mistakes, but I am not a bad person. I can fix this."*

One thing that helped immensely was opening up to a close friend about what happened. It was terrifying to admit how bad things were, but talking about my money mess with someone I trust lifted a huge weight off my shoulders. That friend (who became part of my little support circle) reminded me that I wasn't the first nor the last person to face foreclosure. She helped me replace shame with determination. If you have even one supportive person – a friend, family member, mentor, or counselor – consider letting them in on your situation. There's power in knowing you **don't have to face this alone.**

This period was also when I adopted a new rallying cry: *"Every setback is a setup for a comeback."* I must have repeated that line to myself a hundred times a day. It became my mantra carrying me through. Instead of seeing myself as a failure, I started to frame this setback as the beginning of an epic comeback story. Yes, I was at rock bottom. Okay. That just meant there was nowhere to go but up.

Roadmap for Your Comeback

Now, talk is cheap without action. I knew I needed a plan to actually rebuild. So I started by assessing the damage and prioritizing. Here's how to approach your comeback when it feels like everything's fallen apart:

- **Face the Facts:** I gathered all my bills, statements, and financial papers to get a clear picture of what I owed, what resources I had, and what bills were most urgent. It was hard to look at, but you can't fix what you won't face. Make a list of your debts, monthly obligations, and any income or assets you still have. Knowledge is power here.
- **Triage Your Finances:** Just like in an ER, tackle the most critical issues first. Is there an immediate need (like keeping a roof over your head or food on the table)? Focus on that. For me, after the foreclosure, it was securing affordable housing and making sure basic utilities and food were covered. If you're behind on essential bills, call the companies to negotiate payment plans or hardship programs. Many lenders and utility companies have options for those who ask. Prioritize essentials (shelter, food, utilities, basic transportation) and legal obligations. Credit card companies or other creditors can often wait a bit while you stabilize the foundation.
- **Create a Bare-Bones Budget:** Strip your expenses down to the necessities for a while. Think of this as emergency mode. I canceled every non-essential service and paused all "fun" spending. It wasn't forever, just until I got a handle on things. List out the absolute must-pays each month (rent, groceries, meds, etc.) and see what it totals. That becomes the target your income needs to hit. If there's a gap, it's time to look at increasing income or getting help (more on that soon).
- **Communicate & Negotiate:** Don't suffer in silence. I made those awkward phone calls – to my mortgage lender at first (to no avail in that case), to credit card companies, to anyone I owed. I let them know I was going through a hard time and asked about hardship plans. It was humbling, but many creditors offered temporary reduced payments or interest relief once I explained. If you're in over your head, make

the call – the worst they can say is no, but oftentimes you'll find a sympathetic agent who can offer options. Even utility companies sometimes have hardship programs or can delay disconnections if you communicate.

- **Boost Your Income (Even Temporarily):** I started selling items I didn't need – furniture, gadgets, anything to bring in quick cash. I also took on a part-time evening job for a few months. It was exhausting, but I knew it was a temporary push to stop the financial bleeding. Consider side gigs, freelancing, selling stuff on Facebook Marketplace or eBay – even small amounts help. And remember, this hustle is not forever; it's just to get you over the hump. We'll talk more about side hustles in a later chapter, so hang tight for ideas.
- **Build a Small Emergency Fund ASAP:** This might sound crazy when you're just trying to survive, but even saving $500 for emergencies is a game changer. I know because not having even a small cushion was what turned my situation from bad to disastrous. So as soon as I could scrape together any surplus (from cutting costs or extra income), I set it aside in a savings account. That little cushion kept the next crisis from knocking me flat, which is huge for your confidence.

Throughout this process, I kept reminding myself of that mantra – every setback is a setup for a comeback. It wasn't instant, and it definitely wasn't easy, but day by day I saw progress. I went from feeling powerless to feeling *purposeful.* Each paid bill, each tough phone call made, each dollar saved was a brick laid in my comeback foundation.

Strength in Numbers: Don't Go It Alone

Earlier I mentioned looping in a friend as part of my support system. This was critical. We humans aren't meant to go through ordeals alone, and money struggles are no exception. In fact, shame might whisper to you to keep it secret – but shame loses its power when exposed to light and community.

If you can, find an "accountability buddy" for your financial comeback. It could be a trusted friend or family member, or even a support group (there are personal finance forums and communities online full of people digging out of debt or rebuilding after bankruptcy, etc.). My friend would check in on me regularly – not in a nosy way, just in a caring *"How are you holding up? Anything I can help with?"* way. Knowing I would update her on my progress gave me an extra nudge to stay on track. In fact, research shows having regular check-ins with an accountability partner can skyrocket the likelihood of achieving your goals (some studies cite up to 95% success rates with accountability compared to going solo!). So don't underestimate the power of a partner in this.

Whether it's a weekly coffee chat where you both talk honestly about money, or a text when you hit a milestone ("Hey, I paid off that smallest credit card!"), having someone in your corner makes a *world* of difference. Plus, celebrating wins is so much sweeter with a friend who *gets it.*

Rebuilding: Action Steps

Now that we've covered mindset and support, it's time for some action. Here are two concrete steps you can take right away to kickstart your own comeback:

1. **Debt Snowball vs. Debt Avalanche – Pick Your Payoff Strategy:** Decide on a debt payoff plan that motivates you. *The Debt Snowball* means you list your debts and tackle the smallest balance first (while paying minimums on the rest). This gives you a quick win when that smallest debt is gone, which can boost your motivation. *The Debt Avalanche* means you focus on the debt with the highest interest rate first, which saves you more money in the long run. Neither is "right" or "wrong" – it's about what will keep you going. If you crave quick wins, go snowball. If you're more analytical and hate paying extra interest, go avalanche. Once you decide, **print out a simple chart or checklist** for your chosen method and post it somewhere visible. Having a visual to cross off progress can be incredibly motivating as you see your debts start to shrink.
2. **Choose an Accountability Buddy:** As mentioned above, find a trusted person and ask them to be your "comeback accountability buddy." Explain your goals to them and set up a structure for check-

ins – maybe a text once a week, or a coffee date once a month, whatever works. Research backs this up: accountability can dramatically increase your success rate. Knowing someone will ask "Hey, how's the debt payoff going?" can keep you on your toes. And make sure this buddy is someone supportive, not judgmental. Their job is to cheer you on and remind you of your **why,** not to scold you. **Bonus:** You might inspire them to tackle a financial goal alongside you, and then you both win.

By taking these steps – embracing a structured debt payoff plan *and* securing support for your journey – you're actively setting yourself up for a successful comeback. Remember, ***every setback is a setup for a comeback.*** You've done the hardest part by facing the problem head-on. From here on, each action you take is a brick in the new financial foundation you're building. Keep going, stay focused, and never forget that you have the strength to rise again. Your comeback story is just beginning!

Chapter 4

Saving Grace – Building Your Safety Net

Core Purpose: Make saving a lifestyle, not a one-time event. We want to hardwire the habit of saving into your routine so that putting money aside becomes second nature. Why? Because having a financial safety net gives you peace of mind and options when life throws curveballs.

A Startling Statistic: 36% of Americans would struggle to cover an unexpected $400 expense. That's how common it is to feel unprepared for emergencies. By hardwiring saving into your life – treating it like a regular "bill" you pay to *yourself* – you ensure funds are being set aside for future emergencies or opportunities, automatically. Even a modest cushion (around $1,000–$2,000) can significantly reduce stress and improve well-being. The goal of this chapter is to embed the mindset of **"paying yourself first"** so that building your emergency fund becomes second nature, not an afterthought.

Putting aside money regularly might require some initial discipline, but automation and smart planning can make it *almost effortless.* The payoff is huge. Over time, small, regular savings snowball into a robust emergency fund that can cover surprise medical bills, urgent car repairs, or periods of unemployment. Instead of scrambling when life throws a curveball, you'll have a cushion ready – bringing you stability and peace of mind. Ultimately, making saving a lifestyle means future emergencies become inconveniences instead of catastrophes. Think of it as a gift of peace and security to your future self.

Before we move on, let's keep saving in perspective. Saving is the foundation — not the destination. It's the step that builds comfort and breathing room so you can make smarter choices and avoid panic decisions. But saving alone won't create wealth. It's a stabilizer, not a wealth generator. Once you've built your basic cushion, the next level is learning how to grow money through investing, smart use of debt, and strategic planning. We'll explore those later in the book — but for now, focus on giving yourself this first level of security.

Story Beats: Lessons in Saving

(Let's look at a couple of quick stories that illustrate why a safety net matters.)

- **Old-School Stash vs. Modern Savings:** My grandmother used to hide cash in envelopes under her mattress for a rainy day. It gave her a sense of security, knowing that money was right there if needed. But that cash could easily be lost, stolen, or simply lose value over time due to inflation. For example, during periods of high inflation (say 9% a year), $1,000 hidden under a mattress for a year would effectively shrink to about $916 in purchasing power. **Today, we have better options:** instead of hiding money in the house, you can keep your safety net in a secure, **FDIC-insured high-yield savings account** where it's both protected and growing. In a high-yield account, your emergency fund earns interest – so it *grows* rather than shrinks in value, while still remaining readily accessible when needed. In short, Dad or Grandma's old envelope under the mattress has evolved into an online savings account – safer, smarter, and more effective.
- **Crisis with No Cushion vs. Crisis with a Cushion:** Picture this: your car breaks down unexpectedly and the mechanic hands you a repair bill for $900. Scenario 1 – you have **no savings.** Your stomach drops; you might have to put it on a credit card (and stress about paying it off), or beg family for a loan, or go without a car. It's panic and scrambling. Scenario 2 – you have an **emergency fund** with at

least $900 in it. You're not happy about the expense, but you pay the bill right away from your fund. Your panic likely drops by 80% on the spot, knowing you had it covered. You drive away feeling relieved instead of wrecked. The only difference between these scenarios is that safety net you prepared in advance. As many financial experts say, when you have an emergency fund, an emergency becomes *an inconvenience* rather than a disaster. That's "saving grace" in action.

Teaching Segments: How to Build Your Safety Net

- **Pay Yourself First (Automate Your Savings):** One of the most effective ways to make saving a habit is to ***pay yourself first.*** Treat your savings like the first bill you pay each payday. Set up an automatic transfer to a separate savings account every time you get your paycheck. For example, have 5% or 10% of your take-home pay move straight into savings before you touch it for anything else. By moving even a small amount into savings immediately, you are prioritizing your future self. This automation takes willpower out of the equation – it hardwires the behavior. Over time, those regular deposits add up, and you'll be prepared for larger or unexpected expenses without even having to think about it. **Key tip:** keep this emergency fund account separate (and ideally give it a nickname like "Rainy Day Fund" or "Peace of Mind Fund") so you aren't tempted to dip into it for everyday spending.
- **Build Your Emergency Fund in Stages:** You don't have to accumulate a huge emergency fund overnight. Start with a *starter fund* – even saving $500 or $1,000 as an initial goal makes a big difference. This small cushion can cover minor emergencies (like a car tire replacement or an unexpected medical co-pay) and keep you from reaching for a credit card. Next, aim for one month's worth of essential expenses saved up. Hitting that one-month cushion is a significant milestone that provides more protection. From there, gradually build up to three months of expenses saved. Roughly 3 months of living costs in an emergency account gives you a solid safety net for

bigger disruptions like a job loss or major medical issue. (Ultimately, depending on your comfort level and life situation, you might extend this to 6 months or more for maximum security.) Research shows that having at least three to six months of expenses saved is linked to **much** higher financial well-being – it provides an extra boost of confidence and stability beyond a smaller fund. By breaking the process into these tiers – starter fund, 1 month, 3+ months – you can progressively build your safety net without feeling overwhelmed, and you can celebrate each step along the way.

- **Use Sinking Funds for Predictable Expenses:** Not all expenses that drain our wallets are true emergencies. Many are irregular but *predictable* costs – for example, holiday gifts at the end of the year, annual car maintenance or registration fees, back-to-school supplies, or that big vacation you're planning next summer. Instead of being caught off guard and having to raid your emergency fund or rack up debt, plan ahead with **sinking funds:** dedicated mini-savings for specific upcoming needs. A sinking fund means setting aside small amounts regularly for a specific purpose. Unlike your general emergency savings, each sinking fund is earmarked for one goal (say, a "Holiday Gifts" fund, a "Car Repairs" fund, or even a "Joy Fund" for guilt-free splurges). For example, you might put $50 a month into a car repairs fund, $20 a month into a holiday gifts fund, etc. Then, when the expense arrives, the money is sitting there waiting – you don't have to touch your emergency fund or go into debt. Sinking funds bring clarity and calm to your finances: you proactively plan for known upcoming costs. Many banks now let you open multiple savings sub-accounts or "buckets" to easily manage this. Automate transfers to each, just like you do for your main savings. The result is financial flexibility – those predictable expenses become much less stressful because you've already self-funded them, and your true emergency fund remains reserved for genuine emergencies.

Emotional Touch-Points: The Why Behind Saving

- **"Future-You Deserves Peace."** Every dollar you save today is a gift to your future self. Instead of viewing saving as a sacrifice, think of it as **buying peace of mind** for the "you" of tomorrow. When an emergency strikes, future-you will breathe a sigh of relief and silently *thank* present-you for having the foresight to prepare. (Trust me, I've had that feeling of relief, and it's priceless.) Over half of people say that having money in savings brings them peace of mind – it's a deep comfort knowing that you've "got your own back." Remind yourself that you **deserve** the peace and security that come with a financial cushion. Saving is an act of self-care: future-you is counting on today-you to build that safety net, and she will be so much calmer and happier because of it.
- **Visualize Crisis vs. Cushion:** A powerful motivator for saving is to clearly picture two opposite scenarios.

  Scenario 1: *Crisis with No Cushion.* You're hit with an unexpected bill (car engine failure, medical emergency, job loss) and have no savings. The anxiety sets in immediately – you scramble to borrow money, rack up credit card debt, or skip other bills to pay this one. You feel panic and helplessness teetering on a financial edge.

  Scenario 2: *Crisis with a Cushion.* The same emergency happens – except this time, you do have a well-funded emergency account. It's still not fun, but instead of panic, you feel confident: you pay the bill from your savings, and life goes on. As one finance author put it, when you have an emergency fund, an emergency is just "an annoying inconvenience" rather than a catastrophe.

  Take a moment to **visualize yourself** in those two situations: the stress of the first and the calm of the second. The stark difference in how you feel is all due to that safety net. Keep that mental picture in mind whenever you're tempted to skip saving; it can inspire you to stay on track because you know exactly which version of yourself you want to be in a crisis.

Actionable & Reflection

- **Open (or Nickname) a Dedicated Emergency Account – Today.**

  If you don't already have a separate account earmarked for emergencies, open one as soon as possible – make it the task you accomplish *today.* It could be a high-yield savings account at an online bank or a savings sub-account at your current bank. Keeping your emergency fund separate from your everyday checking helps prevent accidental spending and draws a clear line: this money is for emergencies only. Once the account is open, give it a nickname in your online banking, such as "Emergency Fund" or "Rainy Day Fund," to reinforce its purpose. (Psychologically, naming accounts after goals can boost motivation; I once nicknamed a savings account "Italy Trip" and seeing that name always made me smile *and* skip unnecessary purchases.) Similarly, labeling your emergency account reminds you that future-you's peace lives there. Watching your "Rainy Day Fund" grow is surprisingly rewarding, and you'll be less likely to raid it for non-emergencies. **Action:** Go set up that account – it often takes just minutes online. If you already have one, double-check that it's clearly designated for emergencies and not mingling with daily funds.

- **Identify One Recurring Bill to Negotiate Down – Then Reroute the Savings:** Look at your monthly bills or subscriptions and pick one that you'll focus on lowering this week. Good candidates: cable or internet, cell phone plan, insurance premiums, even memberships like gym or streaming services. Often a call to customer service, mentioning you're considering canceling or switching, can result in a discount or promo rate. Do a bit of homework on competitor rates or current deals, then call up and *politely ask* for a better price. You might be surprised – successfully negotiating a bill could save you $10, $20, even $50 a month. **Next step:** Capture that savings for your safety net. If you manage to cut $20 from a bill, set up an automatic transfer of that exact $20 each month into your emergency fund (since you were already used to living without it). Over a year, that's $240 extra in your emergency fund, courtesy of one phone call! Make this a habit: systematically optimize one bill at a time, and each time, redirect the freed-up money straight to savings. It's like giving yourself a raise and putting it directly toward your peace of mind.

Reflection: Building an emergency fund isn't just a financial exercise – it's about peace of mind, confidence, and breaking the cycle of stress when life happens. By making saving a lifestyle, automating good habits, and planning ahead, you are creating your own "saving grace." Every small step – every automatic transfer, every negotiated bill, every skipped impulse purchase – is another thread in the safety net you're weaving for yourself. Over time, you'll watch that net grow stronger and wider, and so will your peace of mind. Future-you will thank you a thousand times over for every dollar you set aside today. Start now, keep going, and take pride in the financial protection you're building. With this safety net in place, you can face the future with far less fear and far more freedom.

(Sources: Studies and expert guidelines on emergency funds consistently highlight the importance of saving regularly and automating the process. High-yield savings accounts offer safety plus growth. Naming accounts and celebrating small wins are psychological hacks endorsed by financial coaches to sustain motivation. The 36% statistic is from a Federal Reserve report, underscoring why this chapter matters for so many.)

Chapter 5

Earn Your Worth – Growing Your Career and Income

Career as Your Biggest Asset

Your career is likely your single biggest wealth-building tool – even more than any stock or savings account. The skills, experiences, and reputation you develop can pay dividends over a lifetime. I learned this firsthand when I transitioned from military service to a civilian finance career. After leaving the Air Force, I invested in myself by taking night classes (funded by the GI Bill) to earn an accounting degree. It wasn't easy juggling work, parenting, and school, but that education dramatically boosted my earning potential and opened new doors. The lesson? **Never hesitate to invest in your own skills and education, because *you* are your greatest asset.**

At the same time, it's important to understand that working for someone else — even in a stable, well-paying job — rarely leads to true financial independence or generational wealth. A career can provide stability, but real wealth requires ownership, strategy, and intention. Many people earn six figures and still live paycheck to paycheck because their mindset hasn't shifted from income to impact, from earning to growing. Earning more is only powerful when it's paired with new habits, financial awareness, and a plan to make your money multiply. The goal isn't just a high salary — it's freedom. Think of your job as the launchpad that funds your bigger goals, not the final destination. We'll talk more about how to build beyond employment through entrepreneurship, investing, and leveraging opportunities in later chapters.

Navigating Bold Career Moves

Changing career paths can be daunting, but sometimes a bold leap is exactly what you need for growth. I walked away from the familiarity of military life to pursue higher education, essentially "starting over." Later, I made another pivot – from a steady accounting job to an exciting (and challenging) role as a stockbroker at Edward Jones. Believe me, I felt fear and impostor syndrome with each change. But each transition taught me valuable lessons and unlocked higher income ceilings. Don't be afraid of switching lanes if a new field or role offers more opportunity or better alignment with your passion. Research shows that changing jobs or companies can often lead to significantly higher pay increases (on average 10–13% more, versus maybe 3–5% if you stay put). In my case, the move to a financial advisory role came with a steep learning curve and a bigger paycheck. **The Takeaway:** strategic career moves, even lateral ones, can accelerate your income growth – and you can reinvent yourself at any stage if you stay curious and committed to learning.

Know Your Worth and Ask for It

One of the hardest lessons I learned was to advocate for my worth on the job. Early in my career, I completely bungled a salary negotiation. I meekly asked for a raise, didn't have any data to back myself up, and got turned down flat. It felt humiliating – but it was a hugely important lesson. A mentor took me aside afterward and showed me how to prepare and ask with confidence. Armed with her advice, I tried again at my next review and secured a 20% raise. I realized that asking for what you deserve isn't being pushy – it's being professional. In fact, studies confirm that people (women especially) who negotiate their salaries earn significantly more over their lifetimes than those who don't. Negotiating your pay isn't just about the money; it's about self-advocacy and ensuring your compensation matches your contribution.

So how do you approach that nerve-wracking salary conversation? Start by doing your homework. **Research the market rate** for your role and experience – use salary websites (like Glassdoor, Payscale), talk to recruiters, and tap your network to gather data. Think of it as a "salary scavenger hunt" that arms you with facts about what your skills are worth in the market.

Next, **prepare a script and practice it.** Writing out a brief, step-by-step script can organize your thoughts and calm your nerves. Here's an example framework (adapted from career coaches) for how a raise conversation might go:

1. **Express Gratitude & Set the Stage:** Open with appreciation and context. For example, *"I appreciate the opportunities I've had here in the past two years. I'd like to discuss my role and compensation with you."* This starts positive and lets your manager know what the meeting is about.
2. **Highlight Your Value:** Briefly recap your recent accomplishments and contributions. Remind your boss of the value you've added: *"Over the past year, I led the XYZ project, which resulted in [key result]. I've also taken on additional responsibilities like [abc]."* Essentially, shine a light on how you've grown, saved money, earned money, improved processes, or otherwise benefited the company.
3. **Present Your Market Research:** Now share the salary data you gathered. *"I've researched salaries for similar positions in our industry, and roles like mine are currently in the range of \$X to \$Y. Given my contributions and performance, I believe my compensation should be aligned with that market value."* This shows your request isn't arbitrary – it's grounded in real data.
4. **Make the Ask Clearly:** State exactly what you want. It could be a specific salary number or a percentage increase. Be confident and concise: *"I am requesting a 10% increase in my salary to better reflect my responsibilities and the value I bring to the team."* Then **stop talking** – let the silence do the work while your manager processes. (I know, silence in these moments feels excruciating, but it's powerful. Say your piece, then wait for their response.)

5. **End on a Positive Note:** Regardless of their answer, close professionally. If it's a yes – fantastic! Express your appreciation. If it's a maybe or no, ask what steps you could take to earn a raise in the future or if you can revisit the conversation in a few months. *"I understand if it's not possible right now. I'd love to work on a plan to grow into a higher compensation. What goals should I aim for?"* This shows you're committed and still a team player.

By covering these steps, you present a clear, confident case for why you deserve more. You also make it easier for your manager to say yes (because you've basically given them the talking points to justify it). A few additional tips: time the conversation wisely – ideally after a big win or during performance review season. And practice, practice, practice – do a role-play with a friend or mentor, or even in front of the mirror. The more you rehearse, the more natural and less nervous you'll feel.

Remember, negotiating a raise is a normal part of professional life. Companies expect it, and good managers respect it. You're not "greedy" or "ungrateful" for wanting your pay to match your effort. You're simply ensuring you're fairly valued. As one career guide puts it, knowing how to ask for a raise is essential for career growth. So take a deep breath, **believe in your worth,** and step up to the conversation. You owe it to yourself – and you might just be pleasantly surprised by the outcome.

(Bonus thought: If your current job truly can't or won't compensate you fairly, it might be time to consider other opportunities. Sometimes the best raise you get is the one when you change companies, as harsh as that sounds. But give your employer a chance to value you first – you might be surprised.)

Invest in Relationships and Reputation

While pay and promotions are important, don't overlook the less tangible aspects of growing your career: your relationships and your reputation. In the military, I learned quickly that teamwork and trust were everything. The same is true in the civilian workplace. Cultivate genuine relationships with colleagues, mentors, and even competitors. Your network can open doors to new jobs, partnerships, or clients in the future. And protect your professional reputation like gold – show up on time, meet deadlines, treat others with respect. The world is smaller than you think, and a good reputation will precede you (just as a bad one will). People will often hire or recommend someone they trust and like over someone unknown, sometimes even regardless of slight skill differences.

So volunteer for that project, be the person who follows through, help others succeed too. All these things come back around. I got my role as a stockbroker in part because a former colleague put in a good word when I applied – that colleague knew my work ethic and character, and her referral carried a *lot* of weight. Build those bridges; they often lead to wonderful opportunities down the line.

Multiple Streams of Income

This chapter wouldn't be complete without acknowledging: one of the surest ways to increase financial stability (and eventually build wealth) is to have more than one source of income. Your salary is one stream, but perhaps you have a hobby that could become a side business (we'll dive into side hustles in the next chapter), or you can invest in assets that generate income (like rental property or dividends, more on investing later). For now, just plant this seed: think of income like a table. A table with one leg (a single paycheck) is wobbly; a table with multiple legs is sturdy. In my own life, I eventually cultivated multiple "legs" – a 9-to-5 income, a small side business, and some investment income – which made me feel much more secure. If one leg faltered, the others held me up.

We'll explore concrete ideas soon, but as you grow in your career, also think about how you might diversify where your money comes from. Not only can it increase your income, it can buffer you against job loss or industry downturns. Even within your career, developing a broad skill set can allow you to freelance or consult on the side. The possibilities are endless and exciting.

(In the next chapters, we'll get creative about side hustles and entrepreneurship. Stay tuned! But remember, step one is knowing and growing your value, and not being afraid to ask for what you're worth.)

Chapter 6

The Side Hustle Sisterhood – Creating New Income Streams

I can't count the number of times I heard, "Eva, you should really write a book." Friends, family members, even casual acquaintances would say it with such confidence in my abilities. I'd smile and nod, my heart warming at their faith in me.

But as soon as I was alone, a wave of anxiety would wash over me. *Me? Write a book?* The idea lit a spark of excitement in my soul, but it also stirred up something else — **fear.** A deep, stubborn fear of being truly seen, of putting my story out in the world for anyone to judge or criticize. For a long time, I let that fear stop me from embracing what I now recognize as one of my God-given gifts.

Looking back, I realize I was doing what so many of us do with our talents: I was hiding it under a basket because shining felt too scary.

Have you ever felt that way? Maybe people have pointed out a skill or passion of yours and said, "Girl, you're so good at this, you could make a business out of it," but you just weren't sure you could step into that light. If so, you're not alone. **The Side Hustle Sisterhood** is all about women like us recognizing our natural gifts and finding the courage to create new income streams from those blessings. It's about turning those talents — the ones you might have been tucking away out of fear or self-doubt — into opportunities, **with faith, purpose, and a whole lot of sisterly support.**

Embracing Your Gifts and Passions

Each of us has unique gifts placed inside us — skills, talents, and passions that come so naturally we might even take them for granted. Maybe you have a soothing way with children, a flair for baking cupcakes that friends rave about, or a knack for organizing events down to the last detail. These abilities aren't accidents; I believe they're little seeds of purpose planted in you.

Yet it's easy to overlook our own strengths. We might dismiss them, thinking, "Oh, it's nothing special, anyone can do that," when in truth **not everyone can!** What feels effortless to you might be exactly the thing someone else finds challenging — and *exactly* the thing people would pay you for or benefit from.

I encourage you to pause for a moment and reflect on what comes naturally to you. What do people thank you for or compliment you on most often? Consider the tasks or hobbies that make you feel alive and useful. Those are clues to your God-given gifts.

For me, one gift was writing — I could pour my heart onto paper and connect with others through words. For you, it could be anything from design, teaching, healing practices, budgeting savvy, crafting, or nurturing others. **No gift is too small or "unimportant."** In fact, the things we often downplay about ourselves can be the very talents God intends us to share with the world.

Recognizing your gifts is the first step. Embracing them is the next. Embracing means acknowledging that *yes, these abilities and passions are a meaningful part of me, and they have value.* It means not brushing off that compliment or that inner tug on your heart. Sometimes we hesitate to own our talents because we worry it seems prideful, or we think we're not "expert" enough. But humility doesn't mean denying the good in you. True humility is acknowledging God as the source of your gifts and then stepping up to use them for good. When you say, "Thank you, Lord, for this talent, I will do something positive with it," you're honoring both yourself and your Creator.

Think of the times you've been able to help someone using your skills — how fulfilling was that feeling? That's no coincidence. Our gifts are *meant* to be used. Just like a lamp is meant to shine on a stand and not be hidden under a bowl, your talents are meant to shine in the world (even if it's a little scary at first).

Facing the Fear That Holds You Back

Once you've recognized what your gifts are, often the next hurdle is the fear that creeps in. It might whisper, "You're not ready. You might fail. People will judge you. It's safer to just keep things the way they are." Oh, do I know that voice well! Fear is a natural part of any new venture, especially when it involves putting ourselves out there in new ways. For many of us, the idea of starting a side hustle or new income stream triggers that fear of the unknown, fear of failure, or even fear of success. Yes, sometimes we fear success — because what if it changes how others see us, or how we see ourselves?

In my case, the fear of being seen was my giant roadblock. I worried that if I wrote a book and shared my story and advice, I'd be exposing myself to criticism. *What if people thought I was too something, or not enough something else? What if I made a mistake for all to read?* These "what-ifs" played on repeat in my mind. Maybe you have your own "what-if" playlist that keeps you from moving forward. *What if your baking business flops? What if no one buys your handmade products? What if you start that consulting service and feel like an imposter?*

Here's what I eventually learned and want to share with you: **Don't let fear be the boss of you.** It's okay to feel afraid – it means you care about what you're doing – but you have a say in whether fear calls the shots. One thing that helped me was praying about my fears and asking God for courage. I remember one night literally saying out loud, "God, if You truly gave me this dream to write, give me the strength to do it scared." Little by little, I felt a peace that my story mattered more than my fear. I realized staying hidden was actually robbing others of the light I could offer.

A powerful perspective shift for me was remembering the parable of the talents. In that biblical story, a master gives his servants some talents (which were coins, but think of them as gifts or resources). Two of the servants invested their talents and doubled them, but one was so afraid of losing what he had that he buried his single talent in the ground. When the master returned, he praised the two who had put their gifts to work, but he was disappointed in the servant who let fear stop him from even trying. I often think about that. I don't want to bury what God has placed in me just because I'm scared. And I don't want you to, either. **Your gifts are too precious to hide away.** Even if trying something new carries risks, not using your gifts at all is the bigger loss.

So how do we face fear practically? One approach is to confront those scary "what-if" thoughts with a bold response: *So what if? or Even if that happens, I'll be okay.* For example, *What if I fail?* Well, so what if you do? Failure is not final; it's feedback. You'll learn something and try again another way. *What if people judge me?* Even if someone doesn't get it, there will be others who do, and those are your people. *What if I succeed?* If success brings changes, you will adapt and grow — maybe you'll even inspire others to do the same. Turning those worries around takes away some of their power.

Another strategy is to focus on your *why* — your purpose. Why do you feel the urge to start this side hustle? Maybe you want to provide a better life for your kids, or fund a cause you care about, or simply prove to yourself that you can do it. When I was wrestling with fear about the book, I realized my *why* was to encourage other women with my experiences. That purpose became stronger than my insecurity. Keep your purpose in front of you like a beacon; it will pull you through the nervous moments.

And remember, you don't have to banish fear completely to move forward. You can feel the fear and do it anyway. You might bring that fear along with you for a little while, then gently let it go as you grow more confident. Courage isn't the absence of fear; it's moving forward *despite* it. Every small step you take in spite of fear is a victory. Celebrate those little wins! Made that first phone call to a potential client? **Victory.** Published your online store even though your heart was pounding? **Victory.** Over time, those little brave moments add up, and the fear loses its grip on you.

From Passion to Profit: Starting Your Side Hustle

Alright, sister, let's talk about the practical side of turning those gifts and passions into a new income stream. By now you've likely identified one or two talents or interests that light you up. Maybe it's something creative, or a skill you've honed in your day job that could be freelanced on the side. Whatever it is, it's time to explore how that passion can become a source of income — *without overwhelming your life* or compromising your values.

Start small and simple. You don't have to have a full business plan or quit your day job to begin. In fact, most side hustles start as a tiny seed. Perhaps you begin by offering your service to one client or selling one batch of your homemade goods. Dip your toes in the water. For example, if you have a gift for graphic design, you could start by designing a flyer for your church or a logo for a friend's small business, just to build confidence and word-of-mouth. If baking is your passion, take orders for a couple of cakes for the next holiday and see how you feel. Starting small lets you learn and adjust with lower stakes, and each little success will build your faith in yourself.

Do your research, but don't get stuck in it. It's wise to spend some time learning about the field you're entering. If you want to start an online Etsy shop, for instance, research pricing, shipping methods, and see what similar crafters are doing. If tutoring or consulting is your gig, find out what others charge and what clients expect. Just be careful not to fall into "analysis paralysis" — that sneaky situation where you study and plan endlessly and never actually launch. Gather enough information to feel comfortable, then take the leap and learn the rest as you go. Remember, you don't have to know everything to begin. **Clarity comes from action, not just thought.**

Set aside dedicated time. One of the biggest challenges, especially for us women juggling multiple roles, is finding time for a side hustle. I get it — you might be working full-time, raising children, caring for family, and more. Adding a new project can feel daunting. The key is to start by carving out a small, consistent time slot that's just for your side hustle. It could be one hour in the early morning before the household wakes up, a lunch break a couple times a week, or a Saturday afternoon when the kids are at a friend's house.

Mark it on your calendar as an appointment with yourself. Treat that time as sacred and non-negotiable. It might not seem like much, but even a few hours a week devoted intentionally to your new venture can produce amazing results over time. Think of it as planting and watering that seed consistently — eventually, it will sprout.

Make a simple plan and set achievable goals. You don't need a 50-page business plan for a side hustle, but you do want to give yourself some direction. Jot down a basic plan: What are you offering? Who might want or need it? How will you let them know about it? Start with those questions. Then, set a few small goals for the next month or two. For example: "By the end of this month, I will create a social media page for my services and tell five people about it," or "Within two months, I will have my first paying client." Small goals give you targets to aim for and reasons to celebrate when you hit them.

As you start acting on your plan, remember to keep things doable. You have permission to grow at your own pace. This is your side hustle; it doesn't have to consume your whole life to be valid or successful. In the beginning, progress might look like one small win at a time, and that's perfectly fine. Maybe this week you brainstormed a business name or made a list of products you could offer. Give yourself credit for that. Step by step, you are building something new!

And don't forget to keep track of the money side of things too — after all, this is about creating income. It can be as straightforward as keeping a simple log of any earnings and expenses. Seeing even a few dollars come in from something you created can be incredibly empowering. It's a tangible sign that your gift is making room for you.

Sisters Lifting Each Other Up

A beautiful thing happens when women pursue their passions and dreams: other women are inspired to do the same. That's the heart of the Side Hustle Sisterhood. You are not doing this alone. Remember earlier when I mentioned how friends would tell me I should write a book? It was their encouragement, repeated over the years, that finally helped me push past my fear. There's a reason we're focusing on *sisterhood* — because we truly need each other on this journey.

In the often competitive world of business, I believe we can choose a different path: one of collaboration and mutual support. When one sister succeeds, it doesn't diminish anyone else's light; in fact, it shines a path for others. So don't be afraid to reach out and share what you're doing. Tell your trusted girlfriends or family members about your side hustle goals. The people who love you will likely cheer you on — and you may find some of them have resources or contacts to help you. For example, your cousin might know someone who's looking for exactly the service you offer, or your friend from church might volunteer to watch the kids while you host your first workshop. You won't know what support is available until you put your dreams out there.

Find or create an accountability circle. This can be as simple as a monthly coffee date with a fellow entrepreneur friend where you both compare notes on progress, or a small group chat where a few of you share weekly goals and motivate each other. I have a dear friend who started her own marketing side business around the same time I was outlining my book. We decided to check in with each other every Friday. Some weeks, the check-in was just "How are you feeling about everything?" Other weeks it was "What's one thing you accomplished this week, and what's your focus for next week?" Knowing I had to tell someone helped me stay on track, and knowing she was bravely pushing forward inspired me to do the same. We prayed for each other and celebrated each other's wins. That kind of sisterly accountability is pure gold.

Don't have a group yet? Think about a couple of women you know who also have entrepreneurial dreams or who are simply positive, motivating influences. Invite them to be part of a support circle. You might be surprised — others are often longing for the same connection and encouragement that you are. If in-person meetups are tough to arrange, consider an online community. There are many groups on social media dedicated to women in business or specific side hustle niches. Just be sure any group you join feels aligned with your values and lifts you up. Negative or overly competitive vibes have no place in your support system.

Lastly, as you grow in your journey, *be* that encourager for someone else. When you meet a fellow sister with a vision, be the one who says, "I see your gift. You can do this." Sometimes a single sentence of sincere encouragement can spark a transformation in someone's life. We rise higher when we lift others up along with us.

Leveling Up: Guidance for the Seasoned Side-Hustler

You might be reading this chapter and thinking, "Well, I've already got a side hustle going, maybe even a full-fledged business. What about me?" First of all — congratulations on the progress you've made! Even if you're further along, the journey of creating income streams is ongoing, and there's always a next step or a new level of growth (and yes, sometimes new fears to face at each level). Here are a few thoughts for you, dear seasoned sister:

Consider diversification or scaling. If you have one steady income stream, is there a way to expand it or add another related stream? For instance, if you've been tutoring students one-on-one and there's more demand than you can handle, perhaps it's time to create a group workshop or an online course to reach more people at once. If your side hustle has been selling handmade jewelry, could you expand by teaching a jewelry-making class or writing a little e-book on crafting? Think creatively about how your existing platform could serve more people (and earn more income) without necessarily requiring double the effort. This is working *smarter,* not just harder.

Refine your brand and focus. As we grow, sometimes our vision clarifies or changes. Take some time to reflect: Is your side hustle still aligned with your passion and values? As you gain experience, you might discover a particular niche or specialty that really resonates with you and your customers. Don't be afraid to pivot or refine your offerings to match where your heart (and the market) are leading you. The beauty of a small venture is that it can evolve with you; you're never stuck in one format. Staying true to your core purpose while adapting to what you've learned will keep your business both authentic and fresh.

Build a support team. When you start hitting your stride, remember you don't have to do everything alone. Maybe it's time to outsource a task or two that drains you (it could be bookkeeping, administrative work, or social media marketing) so you can focus on the parts of the business you love and excel at. Perhaps you could even collaborate with another woman whose skills complement yours, forming a partnership that benefits you both. Delegating or partnering isn't a sign of weakness — it's a sign of growth and wisdom. It allows you to operate in your zone of genius more of the time, which often means better results *and* more joy.

Keep the faith and stay open to learning. Just because you're experienced now doesn't mean the journey will be free of challenges. You might hit new obstacles or plateaus. In those moments, lean on the same principles that got you this far: trust in your purpose, seek guidance (I often pray for wisdom when I hit a wall), and reach out to your sisterhood. Stay humble and teachable; there's always something new to learn in the ever-changing landscape of business. Perhaps consider mentoring someone less experienced — teaching can solidify your own knowledge and rekindle your passion. And when in doubt, return to your *why*. That core purpose that set you on this path will continue to be your north star through each evolution of your journey.

Whether you're just starting out or already well on your way, remember that creating new income streams is as much about personal growth as it is about money. Every stage is an opportunity to become more fully the woman God created you to be — resourceful, resilient, and generous.

Reflection Questions

As we wrap up this chapter, I invite you to take a moment to reflect on what we've explored. Grab your journal or simply ponder these questions, and be honest and compassionate with yourself as you do:

- What is one natural gift or passion you have that you've been hesitant to share with the world, and what has held you back from embracing it?
- Imagine moving forward despite your fears: what is one small step you could take this week to start (or grow) a side hustle based on that gift?

- Who can you reach out to for support or accountability as you embark on this journey? List at least one person or community that comes to mind.
- How will creating a new income stream in this season of your life contribute to your overall goals or well-being (for yourself, your family, or your community)?

Take your time with these reflections. Remember, *the journey of a thousand miles begins with a single step.* You have everything you need to start or continue building something beautiful. Your gifts were planted in you for a reason, and as you step out in faith and sisterhood to cultivate them, you're not just earning extra income — you're growing into an even stronger, more purposeful version of yourself. I'm cheering you on every step of the way, and so are all your sisters in spirit. **You've got this!**

Chapter 7

Failing Forward – My Entrepreneurship Journey

No entrepreneurship journey is without bumps. In fact, the only guarantee when you chase a dream or start a business is that you **will** stumble a few times. This chapter is about normalizing those setbacks, learning from them, and continuing forward with even more wisdom.

My faith has taught me something crucial about those bumps in the road: they're not there to destroy you, but to develop you. Whenever a venture fell apart, I leaned into prayer and reflection, trusting that there was a purpose in the detour. That perspective didn't erase the disappointment of failure, but it gave me hope. I began to see each stumble not as the end of the road, but as a lesson from God and a stepping stone on the way to something better.

I've shared some of my side hustle stories – the wins and the flops. Now let's dig deeper into what those "failures" taught me, and how they set me up for later success. Think of it as getting cozy with failure and realizing it's not a monster at all, just a mentor in disguise.

Over the Years, Many Ventures...

By now you know a bit of my track record: I once **launched a clothing line** that ultimately failed. Let me tell you, I poured my heart into that project. I was so obsessed with getting everything *perfect* – from the fabric quality to the logo design – that I overprepared and overextended before truly testing the waters. I invested in hundreds of items of inventory because I wanted to be **100% ready** for any customer... and I ended up with boxes of unsold clothes. My perfectionism kept me from taking small, experimental steps; instead I took one giant leap that fell flat. That failure hurt deeply. I felt embarrassed (as I'll share more in a moment), and for a while I saw it as a personal defeat. But in hindsight, the clothing line taught me one of my greatest entrepreneurial lessons: it's good to be prepared, but you'll rarely ever be *completely* ready. Taking **small steps** is so much better than taking none at all. You can always improve things as you go, but only if you start in the first place.

Not every venture of mine was a flop. I had a **small publishing project** that *modestly* succeeded – nothing life-changing, but it proved to me that even a tiny win is still a win. That experience gave me a spark of confidence: a reminder that I *could* create something that resonated with people (even if the audience was small). It taught me the value of starting modestly and growing from there. There were other little projects over the years, too – some that never made it past the idea stage and some that launched but didn't last. Each one added another chapter to my entrepreneurship story.

I also once tried to start a **financial coaching service,** because I love talking about this stuff and wanted to help others with their money. I did get a few clients and tasted what it's like to directly coach people. But I quickly realized that doing one-on-one coaching on top of a full-time job **and** parenting a toddler was burning me out. I was stretched too thin, trying to do it all. Eventually, I had to press pause on that venture and rethink how I wanted to help people with finances (hello, writing a book instead!). Stepping back from coaching felt like a personal failure at first – I hate quitting anything – but it was really a strategic retreat. I learned that sometimes you have to revise your plans to protect your well-being. In this case, it meant finding a **different** way to pursue my passion that better fit my life. Trading evening coaching calls for late-night writing sessions was a tough pivot, but it led me to create the book you're reading now, which reaches so many more people without sacrificing my sanity.

Every venture – whether you'd label it a success or a failure – added to my experience. I even keep a little folder of what I playfully call my **"failure receipts,"** filled with notes about what went wrong and what I learned each time. One thing became crystal clear: entrepreneurship is as much a personal growth journey as it is a business journey. It will test your patience, your resilience, and your creativity. With each project, I wasn't just building a business – I was **building myself.** The failures toughened my skin and sharpened my savvy, while the wins (even the small ones) bolstered my faith that I was on the right path. In the moment, a failed venture can feel like the end of the world, but looking back, I see how each misstep prepared me for something bigger and made me stronger for the road ahead.

Lean into Lean Startups

One concept that really changed how I approach new ideas is the **"lean startup"** approach. In a nutshell, it goes like this: **Build – Measure – Learn (repeat).** Instead of spending a ton of time and money trying to perfect a product or business plan upfront, you put out a *minimum viable* version of your idea quickly (build), see how people respond (measure), and learn from that feedback so you can iterate or pivot as needed. In other words, you start *small and fast,* then refine as you go. This approach embraces the fact that you can't foresee everything and you'll never have it all figured out at the start. I wish I'd understood that sooner! For a long time, I was stuck in the mindset that I needed everything to be in perfect order before I dared put my ideas out into the world. But in reality, you can **never be 100% prepared** for business (or life). There will always be something you only figure out by doing. Now I know: taking one small imperfect step forward beats standing still in pursuit of perfection.

Had I applied the lean startup mentality to my clothing venture, I would have done things very differently. I might have made just a few sample pieces and tested people's interest – say, by taking pre-orders or gathering feedback – **before** ordering boxes of inventory that no one had specifically asked for. Instead, I did the opposite: I invested in a full product line without validating if there was enough demand. *Lesson learned!* These days, I approach any new idea by first asking myself, "What's the smallest, cheapest way I could test this out?" It might be as simple as posting a survey on social media, creating a one-page website to gauge interest, or running a one-month pilot program. By building a tiny version of the dream and getting real input, I save myself from pouring time and money into something that might need tweaking (or scrapping altogether). It's like taking a project for a **test drive** instead of committing to the full cross-country road trip on day one.

Another big lesson I picked up along the way: **separate your business and personal finances** – strictly. When I started side-hustling more seriously, one of the first practical things I did was open a separate bank account just for my business income and expenses. This helped me in a couple of ways. For one, come tax time it made my life so much easier because all my business transactions were in one place (no more combing through personal statements to figure out which expenses were for my Etsy shop vs. my groceries!). Just as important, though, was the psychological benefit: once I had a dedicated business account, any money I spent on my venture felt less like *"my money"* and more like *"business investment."* That mental separation was huge for my peace of mind. It protected my personal sense of financial security and kept me from accidentally overspending on a whim just because my business funds and household funds were all tangled up together. If you're side hustling, I can't recommend this enough – even if your business is tiny, treat it with the respect of its own little financial world. It will make you feel more legit and in control.

I also established some **ground rules** for myself on when to pivot or close a venture altogether. For example, if a side business was consistently losing money or causing me disproportionate stress after a certain number of months, I'd force myself to step back and either change something significant or decide to close it down. It's important to know when to call it quits. It's absolutely okay to say, "This isn't working for me," and move on – that's not quitting in shame; that's being **strategic** with your energy and resources. In the same spirit, I learned to be honest about what kinds of business models or methods just aren't a good fit for *me* personally. For instance, I discovered early on that **door-to-door sales** is *not* my cup of tea – the very idea of going door to door makes my stomach flip. So if I'm brainstorming a new business idea and I realize it would require a lot of cold knocking on doors, I already know it's likely **not for me,** and that's alright. We each have our own strengths and comfort zones. Recognizing what doesn't suit you isn't a weakness – it's wisdom. It frees you to focus on approaches that *do* align with your strengths, so you won't be forcing yourself into a role that makes you miserable. Remember, doing business *your* way (the honest, authentic way) is how you'll find both success **and** satisfaction.

Embrace Vulnerability & Community

One of the hardest things about failing – especially failing **publicly** – is dealing with the embarrassment. I definitely felt that sting when I had to haul dozens of boxes of unsold merchandise from my failed clothing line into a thrift store donation center. I still remember the shame that washed over me that day; my dream literally felt like it was being dumped in a donation bin. I had been so proud of that venture, and here I was getting rid of it like a pile of old junk. In the moment, I wanted to hide and never talk about it again. But something beautiful happened when I finally **opened up** and shared that story with a few of my entrepreneurial friends. To my surprise, they immediately started sharing their own "failure" stories too. We laughed at some of the absurd things we'd each done, we winced in commiseration at the painful parts, and ultimately we **bonded** over these experiences. In that circle of swapped stories, I realized a powerful truth: being vulnerable about the hard parts doesn't make you pathetic or laughable; it makes you **relatable**. It shows others (and yourself) that you're human. I felt such a huge sense of relief to learn I wasn't the only one who had face-planted trying to chase a dream. In fact, one entrepreneur friend told me, "If you haven't failed at least a couple times, you're probably not pushing your boundaries enough." That single sentence shifted my perspective completely. I began to wear my past flops almost like badges of honor – proof that I had dared greatly and lived to tell the tale.

After that, I started a little ritual of **documenting the lessons** I learned whenever something didn't go as planned – those "failure receipts" I mentioned earlier. If a launch flopped or a business idea didn't pan out, I'd sit down with my journal (after I'd finished moping for a bit, of course) and write out answers to a few key questions: *What exactly went wrong? Why do I think it happened? What could I do differently next time? And just as importantly, what went right, despite the overall outcome?* Writing all this down turned something highly emotional (feeling like I failed) into something actionable (a checklist of improvements or ideas for the future). Instead of just stewing in regret or shame, I ended up with a tangible **game plan** for how I'd handle things better moving forward. I cannot overstate how therapeutic this was. It's like taking the power back from the failure – saying, "Okay, you knocked me down, but here's what I'm going to do about it." Over time, I actually came to *cherish* this process. Those scribbled notes in my failure receipts folder became priceless. They were evidence that even in the losses, I was gaining something – wisdom, resilience, insight. It gave me confidence that no failure was final, as long as I harvested a lesson from it.

I also made it a point to find at least one **mentor or "biz bestie"** – someone I could call when I was doubting myself or needed advice on my next move. Going it alone is not only lonely, it's usually less effective. Why struggle in isolation when someone out there has been through the exact same challenge and come out the other side? I'm so grateful for the women (and men) who became my go-to business confidants. Sometimes it was an experienced business owner who kindly took me under her wing for a while; other times it was a peer at a similar stage as me, where we could trade notes and pep talks. I found one of my best cheerleaders through a local chapter of SCORE (a free small-business mentorship network), and I met another amazing accountability partner in a Facebook group for female entrepreneurs. However you find them, **seek out your people.** Trust me, it makes all the difference. We'd schedule monthly coffee meetups or Zoom check-ins to swap updates – "Hey, how did your product launch go?" or "Any progress on that website you were building?" We'd celebrate each other's wins, even the tiny ones like "I got my first Etsy sale!" And when one of us hit a wall of frustration or was ready to throw in the towel, the other would be right there with encouragement and fresh ideas. Having that kind of support network kept me sane and motivated on the rough days. It's such a relief knowing I have someone I can text or call who **"gets it"** – someone who won't judge me if I say "ugh, I only sold one item this week and I'm so discouraged," because they've been there, too. If you're pursuing any entrepreneurial venture, do yourself a favor and find at least one trusted ally. It's like having a spotter at the gym – you can lift heavy things alone, but it's a whole lot safer (and more fun) when someone's beside you saying "you got this!" and ready to help if you stumble.

Action Steps for Aspiring Entrepreneurs:

Now that we've unpacked some stories and lessons, let's get practical. Here are a few action steps and strategies to help you **fail forward** in your own journey:

- **Worst-Case Planning:** This might sound counterintuitive, but it's a huge help in taming fear. Take a moment to write out your absolute worst-case scenario if your venture doesn't succeed. Be brutally honest with yourself: *"I could lose $X of my savings, I might feel humiliated in front of my family, I may have to go back to my old job,"* etc. Next to each worst-case item, jot down what you **would do** if that happened. Often, you'll find that even the worst outcomes are survivable. For example, *"If I lose $5,000, I can slowly save that back up in a year or two by cutting back on eating out and picking up a side gig,"* or *"If I do feel embarrassed, I'll remind myself that even the most successful CEOs have flops and learned from them."* By literally planning out how you'd handle failure, you take away so much of its scary power. It's like shining a light under the bed to show there's no monster. Seeing that you have a game plan **even if things go wrong** will rob a lot of fear of its bite, and you'll move forward with more confidence.
- **Find a Trusted Mentor or "Biz Bestie":** You don't have to navigate entrepreneurship alone. Identify at least one person who can be a sounding board for your business ideas and challenges. It could be a more experienced business owner who's willing to mentor you, or a peer who's also in the early stages of building something. Reach out and establish a regular check-in – maybe a monthly coffee date or a Zoom call – where you can trade updates, ask questions, brainstorm, and cheer each other on. The key is consistency and honesty. When

you know you have someone in your corner to call upon when you hit a snag, it can keep you from panicking or giving up prematurely. Plus, celebrating each other's wins (even the small ones like "I got my first client!") makes the journey a lot more fun and rewarding. Consider this your accountability partnership as well as your support system. Two minds (or a small mastermind group) are often better than one, and sometimes just hearing "I've been there, and here's what worked for me" from a friend can save you from months of struggle. So go find your biz bestie or mentor – it might end up being one of the greatest assets in your entrepreneurial journey.

- **Know Your Strengths and Outsource Your Weaknesses:** You are not required to be great at *every* aspect of running a business – none of us are. The sooner you're honest with yourself about what you **excel at** and what you **struggle with,** the better. Focus your energy on what you do well, and get help in the areas where you're not as strong. In other words, don't be afraid to **hire out or ask for help** for your weak spots. For example, if marketing or social media isn't your strong suit, consider hiring a social media whiz or enlisting a savvy friend to handle that side of things for you. If you don't yet have the funds to hire professionals, get creative: maybe you can barter services (e.g. you design a logo for a friend's business while they set up your Facebook ads), or tap into your community to find folks who can advise you for free. The point is, you don't have to wear every hat. Trying to do everything yourself can lead to burnout and subpar results. By **surrounding yourself with people who are strong where you are weak,** you'll not only free up time and energy to pour into the parts of the business you *are* passionate about, but you'll also dramatically improve your overall results. Think of it like this: *"If I'm not a numbers person, I'll use an accountant or a bookkeeping app to keep the finances straight,"* or *"If I'm clueless about social media, I'll find someone who loves it to help me out."* There is absolutely no shame in building a team (even a makeshift team of friends/contractors) to support your dream. In fact, it's smart business. Great entrepreneurs recognize where they

shine and where they don't – and they make sure every important role is covered by someone's strength, not by their own struggle.

Each of these elements – normalizing mistakes, planning for the worst, leaning on others, and playing to your strengths – works together to build your **resilience** as an entrepreneur. By expecting that stumbles will happen, you won't be so shocked or defeated when they do. You'll pick yourself up quicker and keep moving. In entrepreneurship, that's the name of the game: *fall seven times, stand up eight.*

Remember: failure is not the opposite of success; it's actually part of success. Every "no" you encounter is bringing you closer to a "yes," and every dud idea is narrowing the path to the idea that *will* work. So keep going, keep learning, and **keep the faith.** Trust that God can use even the setbacks to guide you toward your purpose. Your journey is unfolding exactly as it should, *receipts and all.*

(In the next chapter, we'll pivot from business to personal: specifically, the daily money habits that keep you on track. Think of it as the "routine" that holds everything together.)

Chapter 8

Money Habits and Daily Hustle – Your Financial Routine

Picture this: you have a huge financial goal on the horizon. It might be paying off a mountain of debt or saving up for a down payment on a house. Those big milestones can feel overwhelming, like staring up at a tall mountain with no idea how to climb it. Here's the secret: it's not one giant leap that gets you there – it's **all the small, steady steps you take every day** that add up. This chapter zooms in on the daily and weekly habits that keep your finances running smoothly and move you forward. Big goals (like getting out of debt or buying a home) are actually achieved through tiny actions done consistently, with patience and faith that the little things *do* matter.

I'll admit, I get a little **kick** out of knowing exactly where my money is and what it's doing. (I wasn't always this way – there were years I practically stuck my head in the sand and avoided looking at my bank balance out of fear. Believe me, that only led to more stress!). Nowadays, every Monday morning I have a ritual I **love** – I call it my **Weekly Money Date** – where I review my budget, pay any upcoming bills, and see how I'm tracking toward my goals. It's my dedicated time to *check in* with my money. I usually do it with a hot cup of coffee before the day gets crazy, sometimes even lighting a candle or playing soft music to set the mood. This simple routine gives me a sense of calm and control to start the week. After that half-hour of focus, I feel lighter and more prepared – like I've tidied up an important corner of my life before stepping out into the world.

On days when I'm feeling less disciplined or tempted to overspend, I lean on a **quirky little habit** of mine: I record a quick voice note to myself on my phone when I'm about to make a purchase I'm unsure of. I literally talk myself through the decision. For example, you might catch me whispering to my phone in the store aisle, "Hey Eva, you're standing in Target with a $30 pillow you didn't plan for. What's up? Will this pillow bring you joy 48 hours from now, or would you rather have that $30 in your travel fund?" Then I play it back to myself. Hearing *my own voice* ask those questions snaps me out of autopilot spending. (The store employees might think I'm a bit weird, but who cares – my bank account is happier for it!) Maybe talking to yourself in Target sounds odd, but it **works** for me and always makes me chuckle afterward. The key is finding a little trick to interrupt impulse spending *before* it happens. If recording a voice memo isn't your style, try something else to create that pause. For instance, text a trusted friend for a quick "Do I really need this?" check-in before you hit *buy*. Or carry a note in your wallet with a favorite quote or verse that grounds you (remember that sticky note I mentioned back in Chapter 1, the one on my debit card asking "Do you really need this?" – same idea!). Whatever helps you step out of the rush of the moment and make a mindful choice, embrace it. Those few seconds of reflection can save you from a lot of buyer's remorse and keep your goals on track.

Little rituals like these may seem small, but they **compound powerfully** over time. No ritual is too minor to matter – it's like each tiny brick helping to build a cathedral. Each habit helps align your daily actions with your bigger dreams. So, let's create your personal menu of money habits to support your journey!

Daily, Weekly, and Monthly Check-Ins

Setting a schedule for regular money check-ins is like a secret sauce for staying on top of your finances. You don't need to obsess or peek at your accounts every hour (in fact, please don't – live your life!). But having a few *structured,* planned check-in times will keep you connected and in charge of your money without overwhelming you. Here's a simple routine to consider:

- **Daily 5-Minute Scan:** Every day – maybe while sipping your morning coffee – take five minutes to glance at yesterday's spending. Open up your banking app and review recent transactions: is there anything you don't recognize? How's your balance looking today? This isn't a full budget session, just a *quick pulse check.* It keeps you aware of where your money is going and can catch any issues (like an erroneous charge or fraud) early. Plus, it gently trains your mind to be mindful of your finances each day, the same way a daily devotional or quick workout sets a positive tone.
- **Weekly Money Date:** Pick one day a week for a slightly longer check-in – say about 30 minutes. It could be Sunday evening, Friday at lunch, Monday morning, whatever fits your schedule. During this "money date," update your budget with the week's expenses, pay any upcoming bills, and plan for the week ahead. I like to also reflect during this time: *Did I overspend in any category? Why? Do I need to adjust something for next week or move money around?* By regularly facing the numbers, you prevent those end-of-month shocks where you wonder "How on earth did I spend that much?" Consider making this ritual enjoyable: brew a special tea, play your favorite music, or light a candle while you do it. Treat it like quality **me-time** rather than a chore – you might even start looking forward to it.
- **Monthly Goal Refresh:** Once a month, step back for a big-picture review. Revisit your major goals and see how you're doing. Are you on track to save $X for your emergency fund by year-end? How's the debt payoff progressing in total? This is your moment to **celebrate progress** (even if it's something like "I paid off 5% of my debt – woohoo!" – that's progress worth cheering for) and to recalibrate if needed. Maybe you realize you can bump up your 401(k) contribution now, or maybe you decide you need to dine out less next month to stay on track. Use this check-in to course-correct and stay intentional. I'll often jot down a couple of notes for myself during this monthly reset

and even do a little happy dance for any win, no matter how small. Remember, progress is progress!

These check-ins – especially that weekly date – have been a **game changer** for me. It's like any relationship: communication is key. By "communicating" with your money regularly, you build trust in yourself. You start to replace money anxiety with confidence because there are no scary unknowns lurking – you're staying aware. I used to be the queen of avoidance, ignoring my bank account until something (inevitably) went wrong, like a payment bouncing or a late fee hitting. Not anymore. Regular check-ins broke that cycle of avoidance. Now I know where I stand, and that habit has replaced so much of my old money fear with a sense of *peace.* When you show up consistently for your money, you prove to yourself that you can handle it – and that feeling of trust in your own ability is priceless.

Habit Stacking: Tie Money Chores to Existing Routines

One trick I love for making habits stick is called **"habit stacking."** The idea is simple: you pair a new money habit with something you already do regularly, so it becomes almost automatic. Think of a daily or weekly cue in your life and attach a money task to it. Here are a few examples to spark ideas:

- **Morning Coffee & Budget Review:** If you brew a cup of coffee each morning, let that delicious aroma be your cue to do your 5-minute account check. No coffee until you've peeped at yesterday's spending! (Or sip your coffee *while* you review transactions – that's perfectly fine too.) Linking your money scan to your beloved morning brew makes it feel like just another part of starting your day.
- **Evening Wind-Down:** Maybe each night after brushing your teeth, you take one minute to tally up the day's spending in a notebook or budgeting app. If you're old-school, keep a tiny notepad by your bed and jot down "Spent $X on Y today." It literally takes about 60 seconds, but it heightens your awareness of where your money went while it's still fresh in your mind. Pairing it with an existing bedtime

routine (like teeth-brushing) helps it eventually feel as habitual as washing your face or saying your prayers before sleep.

- **Calendar Cues:** Schedule your Weekly Money Date on your calendar like a recurring meeting with yourself. For example, block out **"Sunday 7pm – Money Date"** and set a reminder alarm. Treat it as *sacred* as a doctor's appointment – non-negotiable time. Over time, it just becomes what you naturally do on Sundays. I know a woman who elevates this routine into something she genuinely looks forward to: every week, when Sunday 7pm rolls around, she puts on a comfy robe, applies a face mask, plays her favorite R&B playlist, and makes it a whole self-care vibe while she reviews her finances. Talk about making a chore feel like a treat!
- **Visual Nudges:** Give yourself visual reminders until the habit sticks. For instance, put a sticky note on your fridge or laptop that says, *"Checked your money today?"* It's a gentle nudge every time you see it. You could also change your phone lock screen to a motivational message about your financial goal or a Bible verse about stewardship that inspires you. Little cues like these catch your attention and bring your focus back to your new habit, especially in the early days when it's not second nature yet.

The beauty of habit stacking is that it piggybacks on routines you already have, making new habits **so much easier** to adopt. By linking a money task to, say, your morning coffee or your nightly unwind, you won't feel like you're adding something cumbersome to your day – it'll just ride along with an activity you're doing anyway. Get creative and find cues that fit your life. Do you always check social media at lunch? Make a rule that you'll also spend two minutes checking your bank balance right after. The goal is to weave financial mindfulness into your everyday life in a seamless way. Soon enough, managing your money will feel as automatic and natural as brushing your teeth or putting on your seatbelt, instead of feeling like a burden or an afterthought.

Budget for Fun: The Fun-Money Envelope

Being disciplined with money doesn't mean *never* having fun – it means planning for fun in a guilt-free way. In fact, one of the best habits I adopted was creating a **"Fun Fund"** each month. It's a simple concept that changed my whole mindset about spending. Here's how it works:

1. **Decide on a Fun Allowance.** Pick a small, fixed amount that you will set aside *specifically* for guilt-free fun each month. Maybe it's $50 or $100 – choose an amount that fits your budget and feels right for your situation. The key is that this money is yours to enjoy however you like, no questions asked. It could cover little treats like a manicure, a new book, a fancy coffee every Friday, or a dinner out with friends. By deciding on this amount upfront, you're giving yourself **permission** to spend it joyfully, and that feels empowering.
2. **Set it Aside.** Once you've picked your fun allowance, physically set it aside. I withdraw that amount in cash and put it in an envelope labeled "Fun Money." You could also create a separate checking sub-account or a savings jar for it – whatever method stops you from dipping into it for other things. I love the envelope method because seeing the cash tangibly helps me pace myself. When the envelope's empty, I know I've used up my fun money for the month. If you're more digital, having a dedicated "fun" account or a budgeting app category works too – just make sure you track it so when it's gone, it's gone until next month. This little boundary actually turns into a fun challenge: how creative can you get with your allotted fun money?
3. **Enjoy It – Guilt-Free!** Here's the best part: *spend your Fun Fund with zero guilt.* When you get the urge to splurge on something purely for enjoyment, you can go ahead and do it **completely guilt-free,** as long as you've got money left in your Fun Fund. Feel like going to the movies or splurging on that cute pair of earrings? If the money is sitting in your fun account (or envelope), enjoy it! Savor the treat knowing you're 100% on budget. And once you've used up that fun money, that's it until next month – which actually makes those treats

more special. You'll find you appreciate them more when they're planned this way, because you're truly present for the joy *without* the shadow of worry that you "shouldn't have spent that."

This habit taught me **balance** in a way I hadn't experienced before. Let me confess: before I started doing this, I tried the extreme route of depriving myself completely. I once put myself on such a tight, joyless budget that I gave myself *zero* room for treats. It didn't last. After a few weeks of saying "no" to every little pleasure, I snapped – one rough day, I went out and blew a couple hundred dollars on random stuff just because I felt so starved for fun. I came home with shopping bags and a head full of regret. That "retail therapy" high wore off fast, and I was left with guilt (and a dent in my budget). I learned the hard way that all work and no play is not a sustainable plan. In the past, I tended to swing between two extremes: **either** I'd deprive myself of every non-essential (and then binge-spend later out of impulse), **or** I'd spend on fun things without tracking and then feel guilty afterward. Neither of those felt good or helped my finances. Now, knowing I have *pre-approved* fun money each month keeps my inner rebel satisfied **and** my overall financial plan intact. I don't feel the urge to rebel and overspend on a whim, because I've lovingly built "treat yourself" into my budget. It's incredible what that does for your mindset – you're not in a punishment mentality with money, you're in a balanced, healthy relationship with it.

Automate and Simplify

I'd be remiss if I didn't mention one of the ultimate habit hacks: **automation**. When it comes to money chores, automating what you can is a game-changer for consistency. We talked earlier about the principle of "pay yourself first" – setting up an automatic transfer to your savings or investment account each time you get paid, so you're consistently building your future. You can extend that same idea to as many bills and expenses as makes sense for you. The fewer things you have to *remember* to do manually, the better. Here are some ways to simplify your financial life through smart automation:

- **Automate Your Bills and Savings:** Take a look at your regular bills (utilities, phone, car payment, insurance, etc.) and see which ones you can put on autopay. Set them to pull from your account *after* your paycheck hits so you're never late. Do the same for savings: set up a recurring transfer, even a small amount, to your savings account or emergency fund every month (or every payday). If you have debts, consider automating at least the minimum payments (or more, if you can) for each of them. This way, you won't accidentally miss a payment and incur late fees or damage your credit. Automation essentially **baby-proofs** your finances – it removes the reliance on human memory (which, if you're like me juggling 100 things, isn't always perfect!). You can always double-check periodically to make sure amounts are correct, but you'll have peace of mind knowing the important stuff is handled in the background.
- **Set Up Alerts for Awareness:** Most banking apps allow you to set up alerts or notifications. I take advantage of these "lazy monitoring" habits to stay informed effortlessly. For example, I get a phone notification if any transaction over a certain amount (in my case, $300) occurs on my credit card. That way, I know right away if there's a big charge I didn't expect (which could indicate fraud or just alert me that a large purchase went through). I also set an alert if my checking account balance falls below a threshold I've set. These little pings on my phone nudge me to pay attention if something needs my eyes, *without* me having to constantly log in and check. Consider what alerts might help you – low balance, big transactions, bill due reminders – and set those up. They act like a safety net, catching your attention only when it's truly needed.

With automation handling the repetitive stuff, you free up mental space for more important things (like focusing on your goals, or frankly just living your life!). It feels amazing to know that bills are getting paid and savings are growing without you having to lift a finger each time. I remember the days before I automated, when I'd have a long list of to-dos like "pay electric bill by the 15th" or "transfer money to savings this Friday" – and I'd inevitably forget one during a busy week. I'd get hit with a late fee or miss an opportunity to save, all because life got hectic. Now, those transfers and payments happen like clockwork. No more 3 A.M. panics wondering if I paid the credit card on time – I trust my systems, and they've got my back.

Finally, remember that **habits take time to cement.** Don't get discouraged if you forget a weekly money date or if you overspend your Fun Fund the first month you try it. Building new habits is a bit of an experiment; it's okay to stumble and tweak as you go. If you miss a day or a week, or something doesn't work for you, step back and think about why. Then adjust and try again. Over a couple of months, these actions will start to feel more natural – they'll be just "what you do" rather than something you have to force yourself to do. Be patient with yourself and *give yourself grace.* Change isn't instantaneous, but consistency will pay off. Every habit that slips, every plan that goes awry, is just a learning opportunity. Instead of beating yourself up, congratulate yourself for noticing and commit to doing a little better tomorrow.

Before we wrap up, I want to mention **one more kind of habit** that yields incredible returns: investing in *yourself.* Every course you take, every book or article you read, every conversation with a mentor or wise friend that stretches your understanding – these add so much value to your financial journey. Personal growth multiplies your capacity for wealth because it builds the mindset, knowledge, and discipline that sustain long-term success. It might not seem like a "money habit" on the surface, but trust me, it's connected. For example, setting aside 20 minutes a day to read a personal finance blog or a chapter of a money book, or listening to a financial podcast while you commute, can steadily expand your knowledge. Attending a free workshop at your community center or church about budgeting or investing, joining a small group of women who discuss finances and encourage each other – these are habits too, and they shape you into a more financially savvy, confident person. I consider these activities an investment in me, and they've paid off in so many ways. **Remember:** *the most profitable asset you'll ever manage is you.* When you pour into improving yourself, whether financially, spiritually, or emotionally, you're building a foundation that all the dollars in your bank account will rest upon. A wiser, more disciplined you can create and sustain the wealth that you're working toward. So never feel guilty about spending time (or even some money) to educate yourself or develop skills – that is one expense that yields *infinite* returns in your life.

Reflection: Now it's your turn. What's one **daily** money habit and one **weekly** money habit you want to start, beginning this week? It could be as small as "write down one thing I spent money on each day" or "review my budget every Sunday night." Write down specifically *what* you'll do and *when* you'll do it, and even what existing routine you can tie it to (hello, habit stacking!). Commit to trying it for one month and see how you feel. My bet? By the end of the month, you'll feel more connected to your money and more empowered by your own consistency. You might even start to crave these little check-ins and routines, because you'll see the peace and confidence they bring. And remember, I'm cheering you on every step of the way – you've got this, sis!

Chapter 9

Credit and Debt – Taming the Two-Headed Monster

Credit and debt often feel like a two-headed monster: one head can help you (credit can be a useful tool), the other can hurt you (debt can spiral if unchecked). In this chapter, we'll demystify credit scores, tackle smart debt payoff, and learn to manage these tools without fear or shame.

THE PSYCHOLOGY OF DEBT AND WHY IT FEELS SO HEAVY

Before we talk about credit scores or repayment strategies, we need to pause and look at the invisible part of debt: the emotional and psychological weight it carries. Debt is never just a number. It is tied to memories, identity, pressure, and experiences that most women were never taught to recognize. Understanding this part matters because you cannot change what you do not understand.

Why Debt Feels Personal for Women

Debt hits differently for women. Many women grow up absorbing the belief that they must manage everything perfectly. When money becomes complicated, it can feel like a personal failure instead of a life circumstance. Instead of saying things got hard, many women quietly say, I should have known better. That internal blame creates emotional weight long before any financial consequence shows up.

Debt affects how you breathe and how you sleep. It shows up in the tightness you feel when you check your bank app or the hesitation you feel before opening a bill. These reactions are not weakness. They are your nervous system responding to something that feels unsafe. Debt threatens stability, and stability is tied to safety. Your body reacts before your mind has a chance to process it.

The Shame and Avoidance Cycle

Shame is one of the strongest emotions connected to debt. Once shame appears, avoidance often follows. It becomes a cycle. You feel ashamed of the debt, so you avoid looking at it. The more you avoid it, the more the problem grows. As the problem grows, the shame deepens. The deeper the shame, the more you want to avoid anything related to money.

Avoidance does not mean you do not care. It means you care so much that it hurts. Many women hide statements in drawers, ignore due dates, or avoid budgeting because facing the truth feels emotionally overwhelming. Avoidance becomes a form of protection, not laziness.

Breaking this cycle does not start with discipline. It starts with compassion. When a woman understands the emotional reason she avoids her finances, the shame loses power.

How Comparison Makes Debt Heavier

Comparison is one of the quietest creators of debt and one of the loudest amplifiers of shame. Social media makes it look as if everyone else is debt free and thriving. You see vacations, home renovations, shopping trips, and perfectly curated lives. What you do not see are the credit card balances, the loans, the medical bills, or the money stress behind those images.

People show their highlights, not their realities.

Some women even take on debt because of comparison. They try to keep up, try not to seem like the friend who is struggling, and try to match the image of success they see online. Then once the debt appears, comparison convinces them they are the only ones drowning.

You are never the only one.

Why Smart Women Still End Up in Debt

Debt is not a reflection of intelligence, discipline, or worthiness. Smart and responsible women end up in debt for many reasons. These reasons often have nothing to do with irresponsibility and everything to do with survival, emotional exhaustion, or lack of financial education.

Some women accumulate debt because of emergencies such as medical bills or sudden job loss. Others carry debt because they were helping family or because they entered adulthood without being taught how interest works. Some take on debt because spending became a source of comfort during stressful seasons. For many women, talking about money was considered impolite, so they grew up with responsibilities but no financial language to navigate them.

Debt is rarely about carelessness. It is about moments when a woman needed support or knowledge and did not have access to either.

How Debt Lives in Your Body

Debt does not only exist on a page or a spreadsheet. It shows up in your body. You might feel it in your shoulders, your jaw, your breath, or your sleep patterns. You might feel it in moments you avoid plans, delay dreams, or tell yourself you will deal with it later. Debt can make even a confident woman doubt her stability. That emotional tension is real, and acknowledging it is the first step toward easing it.

Awareness Is the First Step Out of the Cycle

You cannot build financial progress on top of shame. You can build it on awareness. When you finally say, I have been avoiding this because it scares me, or I was never taught how any of this works, or I made choices because I was overwhelmed, everything starts to shift.

Awareness does not erase responsibility. It strengthens it. When you know why you are stuck, you can choose a better path. You can make decisions through clarity instead of fear.

And now that you understand the emotional foundation of debt, the practical steps ahead will feel easier. Your decisions will come from strength, not shame.

Understanding Credit Scores And Score Models

Before you start learning how to raise your credit score, it helps to understand that there is more than one score and more than one scoring model. Many people think they have one single score that lenders use. The truth is that there are several versions of FICO scores and several versions of Vantage Score, and different lenders use different models depending on the type of loan you apply for. Your credit report stays the same, but the scoring model that reads it may change the number you see.

The most widely used scoring family is the FICO scoring system. Within the FICO system, there are many versions. Some versions are used for general lending, others for auto loans, and others for credit cards. Mortgage lenders use very specific FICO versions that are actually older models. This is why your free credit score from an app may not match the score a lender sees.

Below is a clear list of the major FICO versions and what they are commonly used for:

- **FICO Score 2**

  Used by many mortgage lenders. This version is most often pulled from Experian.

- **FICO Score 4**

  Another mortgage version used by lenders. This version is commonly pulled from TransUnion.

- **FICO Score 5**

  Also a mortgage version. Many lenders pull this from Equifax.

  These three scores, FICO 2, FICO 4, and FICO 5, make up the traditional set used in the mortgage industry. Even though they are older models, most lenders are still required to use them for home loans.

- **FICO Score 8**

  This is the most commonly used version for general lending, including credit cards and personal loans. Many banks and credit card companies use this version to make everyday credit decisions.

- **•FICO Score 9**

  This version is newer and treats medical collections differently. It is becoming more common but is not yet the standard for all lenders.

- **FICO Score 10 and FICO 10T**

  These are the most recent versions. FICO 10T includes trending data, which looks at your balance patterns over time. Although these versions provide more detail, many major lenders have not yet switched to them.

There are also specialized FICO scores for specific industries.

- **FICO Auto Score (versions 2, 4, 5 and 8)**

  Auto lenders use these versions because they are designed to predict the likelihood of repaying an auto loan.

- **FICO Bankcard Score (versions 2, 4, 5 and 8)**

  Credit card lenders use these versions to assess how likely a consumer is to manage credit card debt responsibly.

Understanding these models helps you avoid the confusion that comes from seeing different scores from different apps or lenders. You are not seeing errors. You are seeing different versions measuring the same information in different ways.

Vantage Score And How It Differs From FICO

The second major scoring family is the Vantage Score model, created by the three credit bureaus. Many free credit monitoring apps, credit card companies, and banking apps provide a Vantage Score. This score also ranges from three hundred to eight hundred fifty, but it uses a different formula than FICO.

This is why your Vantage Score might show seven hundred while your FICO may be six hundred twenty. Neither score is wrong. They are simply different models interpreting the same data. When applying for major loans, especially mortgages or auto loans, lenders almost always use FICO versions rather than Vantage Score.

Knowing which type of score you are looking at helps you avoid unnecessary stress or confusion. When in doubt, assume lenders will use a FICO version, especially the mortgage versions listed above.

What Goes Into Your FICO Score

No matter which FICO version a lender uses, the general categories that make up your score remain the same. Understanding these categories gives you control, because you know exactly where to focus your efforts.

- **Payment History (35%)**

  This is the largest part of your score. It reflects whether you pay your accounts on time. Late payments, missed payments, collections, and similar issues live here. Even one late payment can lower your score, especially if it is recent. However, consistent on time payments quickly rebuild a positive history.

- **Amounts Owed (30%)**

  This looks at how much of your available credit you are currently using. This is called credit utilization. If your cards are often near their limits, it may signal financial stress. Lower balances create immediate improvements in this part of your score.

- **Length of Credit History (15%)**

  This considers how long your accounts have been open. Older accounts help because they show long-term experience with credit. Keeping older accounts open, especially those without fees, may help this factor.

- **New Credit (10%)**

  Opening several accounts in a short time or having multiple hard inquiries can make you look risky. A few inquiries are normal. A cluster of them may temporarily lower your score.

- **Credit Mix (10%)**

  This looks at whether you have experience with more than one type of credit such as credit cards, car loans, or student loans. You do not need a mix on purpose, but if you naturally have one it can help a little.

Once you understand these ingredients, credit becomes less intimidating. You can stop feeling judged by a number and start looking at the specific pieces of your financial life that influence it.

Reading and Understanding Your Credit Report

The credit report is the foundation beneath every credit score. If the report contains errors, outdated information, or incomplete data, your score will reflect those mistakes. Most women are never taught how to actually read a credit report, so it often feels overwhelming or intimidating. But once you understand the structure, the sections begin to make sense, and you can see exactly what lenders are seeing when they evaluate you.

A credit report is simply a detailed history of how you have used credit over time. It shows your accounts, your balances, your payment patterns, and any negative marks. There are three major credit bureaus that maintain these reports: Experian, TransUnion, and Equifax. They do not always report the same information because your creditors are not required to report to all three. This is why pulling each report individually matters.

When you look at your credit report, you will notice several major sections. Each one tells you something important about your financial picture and gives you an opportunity to make corrections or improvements.

Personal Information

This section lists your name, Social Security variations, past and present addresses, and any employer information your creditors have on file. While this section does not affect your credit score, it can tell you a lot about whether your report is clean. If you see names, addresses, or employment details that do not belong to you, it could signal an error or even identity theft. Accuracy here matters because these details connect your credit history to you.

Credit Accounts

This is the heart of your report. Each account will show the lender name, the type of account, the credit limit or loan amount, the balance, and your payment history. Payment history is one of the most important factors in your score, so this section reveals your consistency. Look for anything that seems wrong. For example, an account showing late payments you know you made on time or a balance that does not match your records. Errors here can cause major damage but can also be corrected.

Credit Inquiries

There are two types of inquiries. Hard inquiries happen when you apply for credit and can impact your score slightly. Soft inquiries happen when you check your own report or when a company performs a pre-approval check. Soft inquiries do not affect your score. When reading your report, verify that all hard inquiries were truly authorized by you. If you see something unfamiliar, dispute it.

Public Records and Collections

This section lists bankruptcies, tax liens, judgments, or any accounts sent to collections. These items have strong influence on your score and can remain on your report for several years. It is important to verify that every record here is accurate and that any debts listed have the correct status. Many people find collection accounts that were paid years ago but not updated properly. Correcting those errors can significantly boost your credit score.

Why This Matters

Reading your credit report with clarity is a form of financial self-awareness. It helps you understand what story your report is telling and gives you the chance to rewrite it. When you know what is in each section, you gain the power to fix what is inaccurate, improve what needs attention, and plan your next moves with confidence.

You do not have to fear what is inside your report. You simply need to know how to read it. Once you do, your credit report becomes a tool for growth instead of a source of anxiety.

Correcting Errors and Reclaiming Your Accuracy

Once you understand what belongs on your credit reports, the next step is learning what to do when something does not look right. Errors on credit reports are very common. They can include wrong balances, outdated information, duplicate accounts, late payments that were not late, or accounts that do not even belong to you. These errors can lower your score, raise your interest rates, or create unnecessary barriers when you apply for credit. The important thing to know is that you have the legal right to dispute anything that is inaccurate.

Disputing an error does not require a special script or a legal background. You simply point out what is incorrect and ask the bureau to take another look. Each credit bureau has a process in place for this, and they are required to investigate. This is not a fight. It is a correction. You are not asking for a favor. You are asking for accuracy. When you approach it with this mindset, the process feels less intimidating and more empowering.

If something on your report does not look familiar, do not panic. Begin with curiosity rather than fear. Sometimes lenders report information late. Sometimes an account transfers to a new servicer and shows up under a slightly different name. Sometimes clerical errors happen. And sometimes there are real issues such as identity theft. What matters is that you face the report with clarity and confidence.

Think of this step like tidying your financial closet. You do not need to overhaul everything at once. You address one item at a time. Each correction helps create a clearer and more accurate picture of your financial life. It also strengthens your confidence because you learn that you have agency and a voice in this process. You are not at the mercy of mistakes or outdated information. You are allowed to request changes that reflect the truth.

Disputing Items Without the Overwhelm

When you find an error, all you need to do is contact the bureau that lists the incorrect item. You can submit your dispute online, by phone, or by mail. Each bureau provides simple instructions, and you choose the method that feels most comfortable. You do not need to write a complicated letter or quote laws. You simply explain what is wrong and why it needs to be corrected. The bureau will review the information, contact the lender if needed, and update the report once the investigation is complete.

The key is to keep things simple. State what is wrong. Provide any documents that support your claim. Wait for the updated results. This is not a process you need to fear. It is a part of financial self care. When your credit report reflects truth, you gain peace of mind and a clean foundation for your future goals.

Monitoring Your Credit With Confidence

Credit is not something you check once and then forget. It changes as your life changes. Monitoring your credit regularly helps you stay aware of changes, catch errors early, and track your progress as you build or rebuild. You do not need expensive services to do this. Many banks and credit card companies offer free monitoring tools. These tools help you stay informed about new accounts, updated balances, credit score changes, and potential signs of identity theft.

Think of credit monitoring as a gentle way to stay connected to your financial health. You are not obsessing over your score. You are becoming familiar with the patterns and learning what supports your growth. Checking your credit does not hurt your score. It helps you understand yourself better. Aim to check your credit reports once a year and glance at your credit monitoring app every month or so to stay aware of any major changes.

These small habits create a sense of control. They help you build confidence. They remind you that knowledge is power and that you are capable of managing your financial life with clarity and grace.

Debt Management and Payoff Strategies

Once you understand your relationship with debt and you have clarity about how credit works, the next step is learning how to manage what you owe with confidence. Debt becomes much less intimidating when you understand the different tools available to you. When women understand the why, the what, and the how of debt, they stop feeling powerless and begin to move with intention. This section gives you a blend of emotional grounding and practical strategy so you can finally create a debt payoff plan that feels realistic and empowering.

Understanding the Purpose Behind Your Debt

Not all debt functions the same way. High interest consumer debt, such as credit cards, tends to drain your financial energy. Installment loans, such as mortgages or auto loans, come with predictable payments and often support major life milestones. Your goal is to understand the cost of each debt and the role it plays in your financial life. Awareness helps you choose the most effective path forward.

Choosing a Payoff Method That Matches Your Mindset

The most successful debt payoff plans are the ones women stick to. Some women need emotional momentum. Some need mathematical efficiency. Both pathways are valid. You get to choose the method that fits your personality.

The Debt Snowball Method

This method focuses on paying off the smallest balance first. You make minimum payments on all debts, then direct any extra money toward the smallest debt until it is gone. Once that debt is eliminated, the amount you were paying rolls into the next smallest. Women who need quick wins to stay motivated often thrive with this method because it builds confidence early.

The Debt Avalanche Method

This method targets the highest interest rate first. You continue paying minimums, then direct extra funds to the debt with the highest interest. This method saves the most money over time. It may feel slow at first, but it is financially efficient and effective for long term discipline.

The Hybrid Method

This method blends both approaches. You may choose a small balance first to create momentum, then switch to the highest interest debt. Many women prefer this because it honors both emotional motivation and financial strategy.

Creating a Clear Debt Snapshot

Progress begins with clarity. You cannot change what you refuse to face. Listing your debts in one place brings relief, not shame, because it gives you a starting point. Include:

- The creditor
- The balance
- The interest rate

- The minimum payment
- The due date

Seeing everything clearly helps you understand where your money is going and which areas need the most attention.

Lowering the Cost of Your Debt

One of the most practical ways to speed up debt payoff is to reduce how much interest you are paying. Many women do not realize they can lower the cost of their debt simply by asking. Calling a credit card company to request a rate reduction can lower your APR, especially if you have been a consistent customer. If they cannot lower your rate permanently, they might offer a temporary hardship plan or promotional rate.

Reducing interest saves money, but it also shortens the time it takes to become debt free.

Debt Consolidation Options

Debt consolidation can simplify your payments and lower your interest, but it must be approached with clarity. Consolidation is not a quick fix. It is a tool. When used wisely, it creates structure and momentum. When used without discipline, it can create even more debt.

Here are the most common consolidation options and how they work.

Balance Transfer Credit Cards

Some credit card companies offer promotional zero percent introductory rates on balance transfers for a fixed period, often between twelve and eighteen months. You transfer your high interest debt to this new card and pay it aggressively during that promotional period. This option can help you save significantly on interest. You must watch out for transfer fees and avoid using the original credit card again during the payoff period.

Personal Loans

A personal loan consolidates multiple debts into one predictable monthly payment with a fixed interest rate. The goal is for the loan rate to be lower than your credit card rates. This option works well for women who need structure and consistency. It is important to check for origination fees and make sure the repayment term is not unnecessarily long.

Home Equity Loans or Cash Out Refinancing

This option can offer lower interest rates because the loan is secured by your home. However, this comes with a major caution. You are turning unsecured debt into debt that is tied to your house. If something goes wrong, your home is at risk. This option should only be considered after careful thought and a realistic plan for repayment.

What to Watch Out For

Consolidation can be powerful when used with discipline. It can also become dangerous if old habits return. Many women consolidate their debt, clear their credit cards, and then slowly use the cards again. This creates the outcome every woman fears. The original loan plus new credit card balances.

This is why discipline must be part of the conversation. Consolidation gives you the opportunity for a fresh start. It is up to you to protect that fresh start.

Ask yourself:

- Am I willing to stop using credit cards during this payoff period
- Am I committed to following the repayment plan
- Is this option truly saving me money long term

When you answer these questions honestly, you make decisions that support your future instead of repeating your past.

Emotional Sustainability Matters More Than Speed

Debt payoff is not a race. It is a journey that requires consistency and compassion. You will have months where you make progress and months where you need to step back. You might have unexpected expenses that slow you down. None of this means you are failing. It means you are human.

Celebrate every win. A payment made on time is a win. A balance dropping by even ten dollars is a win. A month where you did not add new debt is a win. When you track your progress, you strengthen your confidence.

Debt is not your identity. Debt is a financial situation that you are rewriting one payment at a time.

Using Debt as a Tool: Understanding OPM and Smart Leverage

Once you have mastered the art of managing debt, you are ready to understand something that many wealthy people know instinctively. Not all debt is harmful. Some forms of debt can work for you and help you move forward faster. This is often referred to as OPM, which stands for Other People's Money. Wealthy people use OPM to build assets, create income, reduce certain tax burdens, and expand opportunities. The difference is that they use it with strategy instead of emotion, and intention instead of impulse.

Many women have been conditioned to fear debt. So when the idea of using borrowed money to build wealth comes up, it can feel unsafe or even irresponsible. Before you ever explore OPM, you need to feel grounded in your habits, your clarity, and your emotional stability. That is why we start with mindset before strategy. Strategy without healing will always feel overwhelming.

When used responsibly, OPM becomes a tool that helps you create momentum. A woman might use a mortgage to buy a rental property that produces income. Another might use a business loan to launch something profitable. Someone else might consolidate high interest debt using a lower interest loan to reduce financial stress. These are all examples of using borrowed money to create something that grows.

There is another layer that often gets overlooked, especially among women. Strategic use of OPM can also reduce certain tax liabilities when done correctly. For example, an investment property often allows you to deduct mortgage interest, repairs, depreciation, and other qualified expenses. Business loans used for legitimate operations may allow the interest to be deducted as well. These tax benefits can increase your cash flow and accelerate your financial progress. The goal is not to chase loopholes. The goal is to understand that smart leverage can support both your income building and your long term tax planning.

The Mindset Shift Behind Smart Leverage

Before a woman uses OPM, she checks her motives. Smart leverage comes from preparedness. It comes from a clear plan. It comes from a place of confidence, not pressure. Ask yourself:

- Is this decision creating something valuable or profitable
- Am I emotionally ready to manage the responsibility that comes with borrowing
- Do I have a repayment plan that is realistic
- Does this align with my long term goals
- Am I borrowing from strength instead of fear

If your answers feel steady and grounded, you are ready to explore options. If any answer makes you pause, trust the pause. Pausing is wisdom.

OPM in Everyday Life

Many women already use OPM without realizing it. A mortgage that allows you to purchase an asset that grows in value is a form of leverage. A business loan or line of credit used to expand something profitable is leverage. A home equity loan used to renovate a property that increases in value or cash flow is leverage. These examples use borrowed money to create something that builds your financial life instead of draining it.

The key difference is simple. Smart leverage puts money into something that grows. Harmful debt pulls money away from your present and your peace.

Borrowed money should work for you, not against you. It should build stability, options, and long term benefit. It should never be based on a hope that "one day" something might pay off. Smart leverage is grounded in reality, not possibility.

The Emotional Responsibility That Comes With Leverage

Any use of OPM requires emotional maturity. You need the discipline you have been building throughout this book. You need the clarity you gained from understanding your credit. You need the trust you rebuilt within yourself while healing your money story.

Leverage magnifies whatever foundation it sits on. If your foundation is stable, leverage expands your opportunities. If your foundation is fear based, leverage expands the fear.

This is why foundation matters. This is why timing matters. This is why self trust matters.

A Woman Centered Approach to OPM

Many financial books discuss OPM in a cold technical way, but that is not how women make decisions. Women consider peace. Women consider responsibility. Women consider long term impact. A feminine approach to leverage honors emotional wellbeing, grounded wisdom, and spiritual alignment.

Before you borrow to invest, ask yourself how you want to feel. Confident. Calm. Steady. Secure. Your emotional clarity is part of your financial clarity. When you are grounded, leverage becomes a tool instead of a burden.

The Gift of Preparedness

Learning to manage debt responsibly prepares you to leverage debt strategically. When you keep promises to yourself, pay bills on time, reduce balances, and build healthy habits, you are strengthening the emotional muscles that make smart leverage possible. You are preparing yourself to make bigger decisions from a place of confidence.

Your future self will thank you. She will not fear debt. She will understand it. She will use it intentionally. She will understand the advantage of letting borrowed money help her build assets, increase cash flow, and reduce certain taxes in legally sound ways. She will have options because you built the foundation.

She will be capable of so much more than survival. She will be ready for expansion.

Stepping Into Your Financial Strength

You have walked through a lot in this chapter, and it is important to pause and acknowledge that. You explored the emotional side of debt and the way shame, comparison, and past experiences can quietly shape your decisions. You learned how credit actually works and what lenders look for, and you gained clarity around the numbers that once felt intimidating. You also explored practical strategies for paying down debt, evaluating consolidation, lowering interest rates, and even using money with intention to create opportunities in the future. All of that knowledge was meant to give you a sense of direction rather than overwhelm you.

Now that you have this information in your hands, I want you to understand something very clearly. Debt is not a reflection of your character. It is not a sign that you are irresponsible or unworthy. It is simply a circumstance that can be changed with understanding, patience, and structure. Many of the decisions you made in the past were shaped by the version of yourself who was doing the best she could with the knowledge, resources, and emotional capacity she had at the time. There is no shame in that. Growth begins when you give yourself permission to release judgment and choose differently from this moment forward.

Rebuilding your financial life is really about rebuilding trust with yourself. Every time you face a number that you used to avoid, you strengthen that trust.

Every time you choose clarity instead of panic, you reinforce your confidence. Every step you take, whether it feels big or small, is part of your progress. You do not need perfection. You simply need consistency and compassion for yourself as you learn new habits and unlearn the patterns that no longer serve you.

Your next step does not have to be dramatic. It can be something simple, like checking your credit report without bracing for the worst, or making one extra payment toward a balance, or choosing to pause before spending out of stress. It might mean sharing your financial truth with someone who makes you feel safe, or reminding yourself that you deserve a sense of ease with money. Small steps create momentum, and momentum creates change.

As you continue on this journey, I want you to remember that your financial power grows the moment you decide to take ownership of your story. You are capable of learning new skills. You are capable of correcting what needs to be corrected. You are capable of building a future that feels steady, intentional, and grounded. Nothing in your past has disqualified you. You are not defined by your debt, your score, or the moments when you felt lost. You are defined by the choices you are making now and the woman you are becoming.

Your comeback has already begun. As you move into the next chapter, carry with you the understanding that you are stronger than you realize, wiser than you give yourself credit for, and absolutely worthy of a financial life that brings you calm and confidence.

Chapter 10

Investing Made Simple – Let Your Money Grow

Starting to invest can feel daunting, but even small, patient steps add up in a big way over time. Imagine you buy a stock or contribute to your 401(k) and the market dips the next month – it might feel like you "lost" money. But instead of panicking, you stay the course, maybe even buy a bit more while prices are low. Over time, markets historically recover and grow, and your investments can increase substantially. Research confirms that people who sell in a panic during downturns often lock in losses, while disciplined, long-term investors who **stay invested** tend to benefit when the market rebounds. The simple act of investing consistently and not reacting out of fear is a proven recipe for wealth-building.

This chapter is all about making the concept of investing approachable. You don't need to be a Wall Street expert to let your money work for you. Even if you start with $50 a month, the key is to start **somewhere** and be consistent.

And here's the truth: you don't need a lot of money to start investing — you just need to start. Even small, consistent contributions grow over time through the power of compounding. Wealth isn't built from one big deposit; it's built from steady, faithful action. Every small investment is a seed. Time and consistency are what make it grow.

The Power of Compounding

You might have heard Albert Einstein reportedly called compounding "the eighth wonder of the world." Compounding is basically earning money on your money. For example, say you invest $1,000 in an index fund (we'll explain those in a minute) and it earns an average of 7% per year. After the first year, you have $1,070 (your original plus $70 gain). If you leave that alone, the next year you earn 7% on $1,070 (not just on the $1,000) which is about $75, making your total ~$1,145. Each year, the earnings get a little bigger because your base is growing. Fast forward 30 years, and that $1,000 could grow to around $7,600 without you adding a single extra penny, thanks entirely to compounding. **Now imagine** you were adding a little bit consistently to that investment – the growth becomes exponential.

The Takeaway: time in the market matters more than timing the market. The earlier and longer you can invest (even with small amounts), the more compounding can work its magic.

Account Types: Retirement vs. General Investing

Different accounts serve different goals, and they also come with different tax benefits. Here are the big ones:

- **401(k) or 403(b):** These are employer-sponsored retirement plans. If you have one at work, definitely consider contributing – especially if your employer offers a match (that's free money!). Contributions are often pre-tax (meaning you don't pay income tax on the money you put in now; you'll pay when you withdraw in retirement). There are also Roth 401(k) options some employers offer (taxed now, tax-free later). The big advantage is automation (comes out of your paycheck) and higher contribution limits than IRAs.
- **IRA (Traditional or Roth):** An IRA is an Individual Retirement Account you open yourself (banks or brokerages can help you set one up easily online). A **Traditional IRA** is similar to a 401k in that contributions can be pre-tax (reducing your taxable income now, but taxed on withdrawal). A **Roth IRA** is my personal favorite if you

qualify (there are income limits): you contribute post-tax money (no immediate tax break) but then it grows tax-free, and in retirement, withdrawals are tax-free. Imagine not paying a dime of tax on decades of investment gains – yes please! For 2025, you can contribute up to $6,500 per year to an IRA (or $7,500 if you're over 50).

- **Brokerage Account:** This is a general, taxable investment account with no special tax advantages. You put money in after tax, invest it how you like, and you pay taxes on dividends, interest, or profits each year (or when you sell). The advantage here is flexibility – you can withdraw money at any time (though be mindful of taxes and potential penalties on gains held under a year). This is great for investing money you might want before retirement age or above what you can put in retirement accounts. There's no contribution limit.

The strategy many follow is: contribute enough to your 401k to get any employer match (never leave that on the table!), then max out a Roth IRA if you can, and if you still have more to invest, go back to the 401k up to its limit, and/or use a brokerage for non-retirement goals.

Diversify: Funds vs. Individual Stocks

One principle of sane investing is **diversification** – basically, *don't put all your eggs in one basket.* Instead of betting on a single company's stock and hoping it soars (or risking it sinks), you spread your money across many investments to reduce risk.

The easiest way to diversify when starting out is through **mutual funds or ETFs (exchange-traded funds),** especially index funds. An index fund is like a basket that holds a tiny piece of *every* stock in a certain index. For example, an S&P 500 index fund lets you own a slice of all 500 of the largest US companies at once. If one company has a bad year, it's buffered by others that might be doing well. Index funds typically have low fees and historically, the S&P 500 has returned around 7-8% annually over the long term (though remember: past performance isn't a guarantee of future results, but it's a decent reference point).

So for a beginner, buying, say, a **Total Market Index Fund** or an **S&P 500 ETF** is a simple way to "invest in the stock market" without having to pick stocks. You can also diversify across types of investments – for example, also holding some bonds via a bond fund (bonds are generally lower risk, lower return, good for stability especially as you get closer to needing the money).

If you're very conservative, you might tilt more of your portfolio to bonds; if you're young and have a long horizon, you might go mostly stocks via funds.

A quick note on risk and tolerance: Stocks will fluctuate – that's their nature. The price of your fund will go up and down daily. But if you're investing for a goal that's years or decades away, you ride those waves. Over time, historically, the trend has been upward. If seeing fluctuations freaks you out, start with small amounts until you get comfortable.

(And remember, if you already contribute to a retirement plan, you are likely invested in funds within that plan. Take a peek at your allocations there – it can be a learning experience to see how that money is invested.)

"You already invest – in everyone else. Time to invest in you." This saying resonates with me, because as women we often invest energy and money in our families, communities, employers. But building wealth means directing some of that investing energy into ourselves and our future.

Take Action: Your Next Steps

- **If you haven't started investing yet, open an account.** If your job offers a retirement plan, enroll in it. If you can swing it, contribute at least enough to get the match (common matches are like "we match 50% of your contribution up to 6% of your salary" – that means if you put in 6% of pay, they add 3%). If you don't have a retirement plan at work, consider opening an IRA. Most online brokerage platforms (Vanguard, Fidelity, Schwab, etc.) make it easy with step-by-step guidance.
- **Automate your contributions.** Increase your 401(k) or IRA contribution by at least 1% of your pay (or set up an automatic monthly transfer to your IRA or brokerage). A little bump today

can become a large sum later thanks to compounding. Many experts suggest aiming to save 10-15% of your income for retirement, but if you're not there yet, any increase is good. There's a concept of "auto-escalation" – some plans even do this for you – where you increase your contributions by 1% each year. You barely feel it, and it significantly boosts your nest egg over time.

- **Learn on-the-go.** You don't need to know everything to start, but commit to learning a bit as you go. Maybe listen to one investing podcast this week (I love ones like *HerMoney with Jean Chatzky* or *Brown Ambition,* which often discuss investing basics in a friendly way). Or pick up a beginner-friendly book like *"The Simple Path to Wealth"* by J.L. Collins or *"Smart Women Finish Rich"* by David Bach. Podcasts and books are free or low-cost ways to grow your knowledge while commuting, cooking, or relaxing. They've been called "one of the best free resources" for learning market basics on your own time.

By taking these small steps—automating contributions and continuing your financial education—you'll turn hesitation into momentum. Remember that investing is a journey: start now, stay consistent, and let time and smart choices help your money grow. Years from now, you'll look back and be so grateful you began when you did.

(Next, we'll talk about securing the future in a broader sense – legacy, estate planning, and making sure the wealth you build continues to serve your loved ones and community. Onward!)

Chapter 11

The Calm Investor: Building Wealth Without Fear

There is a moment in your financial journey when you shift from simply surviving to quietly building something stronger. It doesn't happen with fireworks or big announcements. It happens in a whisper. A moment of clarity. A moment of courage. A moment when you realize:

"I want my money to grow even when I'm not touching it."

That moment — the moment you step into investing — is often where fear tries to creep in. For many women, the stock market feels like a world built for someone else. A world of fast-talking men on Wall Street, complicated numbers running across screens, charts and graphs and opinions flying everywhere. A world that seems unpredictable. A world that feels unsafe. But that's only because no one taught us the truth in a way that feels like it belongs to us. Investing does not require fearlessness. It requires calm. It requires clarity.

It requires a willingness to breathe through uncertainty. It requires knowing that your long-term future is bigger than a short-term dip. And most importantly, it requires trusting yourself more than you trust the noise around you.

This chapter is not here to turn you into a finance expert. It's here to turn you into a calm investor — a woman who understands the market well enough to stay steady, hold her ground, and let her money grow without being shaken by every headline or fluctuation.

Let's walk into this new chapter with confidence, together.

Learning to Read the Market Without Fear

One of the first steps toward becoming a calm investor is understanding the basic rhythm of how the market moves — without letting the technical side intimidate you. Markets are like seasons. They shift. They cool. They heat up. They repeat patterns over and over, even if the details change.

Bull markets and bear markets — told simply

You will hear two words a lot:

A **bull market** is when the market grows with confidence. People are optimistic, businesses are thriving, investments are climbing. Bulls thrust upward — so think of prices rising.

A **bear market** is when the market falls and fear spreads. Investors pull back, news stories sound frightening, and prices drop. Bears swipe downward — so think of prices sinking. Most people hear "bear market" and immediately think "disaster." But a bear market is not the end. It's simply a season. Historically, bear markets last about a year or so. Bull markets often last many years — sometimes five, sometimes six, sometimes longer. And here's the quiet truth nobody says loudly enough: **The market has spent far more time rising than falling.**

If you zoom out over decades, the dips look like little bumps on a long, rising road. But when you zoom in too close — day by day or month by month — those bumps feel like cliffs. This is why calm investors learn to zoom out.

Why Fear Feels So Loud — and Why It's Lying to You

When your investment account drops — even a small amount — your brain interprets it as danger. It doesn't separate temporary volatility from actual loss. It reacts the same way it would if you touched something hot.

This is why even small dips feel personal. Why you might feel anxious or frustrated. Why you might question yourself. Why you might want to pull out, sell everything, or "stop the bleeding." But fear is a short-term storyteller. It only knows "right now." It has no understanding of "long-term."

Becoming a calm investor means gently retraining your mind to understand:

- Dips are normal
- Volatility is expected
- Growth is long-term
- Patience is your advantage
- Fear is not a financial advisor

We are conditioned to believe that "down" means "wrong." But in investing, down is simply part of how the market breathes.

A Real Moment From My Early Career: Watching Fear in Real Time

There is no better example of this than what I witnessed in 2009. At the time, I was brand new — a trainee in a regional financial advisor's office at Edward Jones — still learning how this entire world worked. I didn't have clients. I wasn't advising. I was simply observing, taking notes, absorbing everything I could.

And then the phones started ringing. It was the tail end of the Great Recession. The market was in freefall. People felt like the sky was collapsing on the financial world. I watched grown adults — people who had saved for decades — call the advisor in pure panic. Some were angry. Some were crying. Some were shaking in their voices. The fear was so real you could feel it in the air. "Sell everything." "Take me out of the market." "I can't watch this anymore." "I'm going to lose everything."

Call after call, the panic spread like a virus. I remember sitting there — a young woman at the very beginning of her financial career — watching fear move through people like a tidal wave.

But here's what stayed with me far more than the panic. A handful of clients were calm.

Not because they didn't feel fear — but because they trusted their long-term plan.

They had conversations with the advisor where they asked questions, grounded themselves, and chose patience over panic. They didn't sell. They didn't retreat. They didn't let fear make the decision. And years later, when the market recovered and soared past its previous highs, those calm clients were the ones who benefited the most. Their accounts bounced back. And then they multiplied.

The ones who panicked locked in losses that took years to rebuild, and some never caught up. I wasn't advising then. But I was learning. And the lesson was clear: **panic feels urgent, but patience builds wealth.**

That was the moment I understood what a calm investor really is — not someone who never feels fear, but someone who doesn't let fear drive the entire car.

Why Calm Investors Win (Even If They Don't Feel Like Experts)

One of the biggest myths about investing is that you need to be an expert to do it well. You don't. In fact, experts often get in their own way. Women — especially women who invest consistently and calmly — often outperform their male counterparts over the long term.

Why?

Because women tend to:

- overtrade less
- research more
- stick to their plan
- avoid impulse decisions
- invest consistently
- listen to long-term advice

Calm doesn't mean passive. Calm means intentional.

It means:

- you invest based on strategy, not emotion
- you stay grounded when things get loud
- you understand you're planting seeds, not buying lottery tickets

And most importantly: **You know your money is allowed to grow slowly.**

Let's Talk About Volatility — In Real Human Language

Volatility is just a fancy way of saying the market moves up and down. But here's what nobody tells you:

Volatility is the price of admission for long-term growth.

You cannot get decades of upward return without accepting that some days, the chart will dip. Think about it like flying. Turbulence does not mean the plane is crashing. It means the air is shifting. When the market dips, it's turbulence. Not danger. Not disaster. Not the end of your financial future. Just movement. A calm investor doesn't ignore turbulence — she just doesn't assume it means she's falling out of the sky.

Real-Life Calm Investor Moments (Scenarios That Build the Chapter Naturally)

Scenario 1: The 401(k) Dip That Felt Personal

Maya opened her retirement account during a market downturn. Her balance was lower than the month before, and she immediately thought:

"I'm doing something wrong." She was not. Her investments were simply experiencing a normal cycle.

A year later, her consistency paid off and her account had grown beyond what she ever expected — not because she avoided dips, but because she invested through them.

Scenario 2:
The First-Time Investor Who Felt "Too Late"

Tasha started investing in her 40s. She felt behind. She felt embarrassed. She almost didn't start at all. But consistency (even in small amounts) changed everything. The market rewarded her patience. And she realized the truth:

It's not about when you start. It's about staying in.

Scenario 3:
The Young Mom Who Thought Investing Meant Losing Control

Janelle didn't want to "risk" her money because she was a single mom and needed security. But after learning how diversification works (owning multiple types of investments so one dip doesn't ruin everything), she realized investing actually created security over time — not the opposite.

These are the women your book speaks to. These are the women who keep reading because they feel seen.

What Calm Investors Do Differently

Calm investors don't avoid fear — they understand fear. They also don't glamorize risk — they respect it. Here's how calm investors move differently than others do.

1. They know their time horizon.

Investing for retirement 20 years away is not the same as investing for a house next year. If your goal is long-term, dips mean nothing.

2. They diversify without overthinking it.

They don't put all their money in one stock. They spread it across different types of investments. That alone reduces anxiety.

3. They don't check their accounts constantly.

Calm investors are not glued to their phones. They set a schedule — monthly or quarterly — and stick to it.

4. They contribute consistently, even when the market dips.

Especially when the market dips — because that's when prices are "on sale."

5. They adjust their risk before a storm, not in the middle of one.

If a steep drop would keep you up at night, choose a more balanced portfolio up front. Calm investing is emotional preparedness as much as financial preparation.

Faith Over Fear: The Most Underestimated Investment Tool

Money will always have cycles. Life will always have uncertainty. But your peace does not have to rise and fall with the market. Faith — however you define it — has a way of anchoring you when the numbers feel unsteady.

For some women, faith means trusting that God provides even when the world feels unstable. For others, it means believing that they were created with wisdom and can make sound decisions.

For many, it means remembering that peace is not found in a 401(k), but in the One who provides for your needs.

A gentle scripture reminds us:

"Whoever gathers little by little will increase it." That's investing. That's patience. That's long-term growth.

Another reminds us:

"Don't put your hope in wealth, which is uncertain." It doesn't mean wealth is wrong — it means wealth isn't your foundation. Faith doesn't replace investing. Faith steadies investing. It gives you the courage to stay the course when fear whispers otherwise.

Becoming the Calm Investor

One day, you will look back at your financial journey and see a turning point. A moment when you stopped reacting to every market movement and started trusting your long-term strategy.

A moment when you began investing consistently. A moment when fear quieted. A moment when you realized you don't have to know everything — you just need to stay committed.

A moment when you stopped seeing volatility as a threat and started seeing it as a normal part of the process. That's when you become the calm investor. Not because you knew the perfect strategy. Not because you never felt fear. Not because you timed the market. But because you stayed. You trusted yourself. You trusted your plan. You trusted your growth.

Calm investors build wealth slowly, steadily, quietly. They don't rush. They don't panic.

They don't let fear be their financial advisor. They let consistency be their strategy. They let time be their friend. They let faith be their anchor. And they let their future unfold one investment at a time.

Takeaway

You don't need special knowledge. You don't need a finance degree. You don't need perfect timing. You just need calm. You need clarity. You need courage. And you need a long-term vision you believe in.

Your wealth grows with patience — not perfection.

You're not investing for today. You're investing for the life you're building. The woman you're becoming. The future you deserve. And she — future you — is cheering you on. *You don't need to time the market. You just need time in the market. You are the calm investor now.*

Chapter 12

Your Financial Freedom Milestones: From Surviving to Thriving

Every financial journey is unique, but there are common milestones on the road from just getting by to genuinely thriving. Think of these like stages or levels in your money life — markers that help you understand not only where you are but where you're headed. As you move from one stage to the next, your mindset expands, your confidence grows, and your relationship with money becomes more grounded, calm, and empowered.

The goal here isn't for you to rush or compare. There is no "right age," no perfect timeline, no finish line to chase. Life will pull you forward, set you back, and redirect you at unexpected times. You might spend years in one stage and glide through another. You might revisit a stage you thought you left behind. That's not failure. That's life.

Financial growth is not a straight line — it's a journey of intention.

Real Talk: "You're not behind — you're just getting started with intention."

In this chapter, we'll explore four financial milestones: **Stability, Momentum, Freedom, and Legacy.**

You'll see what each stage looks like in practice, how it feels, and the small, meaningful steps that move you forward.

Let's walk through these stages together.

Stage 1: Stability (Surviving to Standing Strong)

What Stability Really Means

Stability is the first major turning point — the shift from constant struggle to quiet control. It's the stage where you stop reacting to emergencies and start creating a sense of steadiness in your financial life.

Stability isn't flashy. It doesn't always look like success from the outside. But emotionally? It's powerful.

Stability feels like:

- Being able to breathe again
- No longer bracing every time your phone buzzes with a bank alert
- Knowing the bills are paid on time
- Having just enough cushion to avoid panic
- Feeling proud of yourself in new, quiet ways

For many women, Stability is the first time they feel safe around money. It might still be tight. It might still be fragile. But it's no longer chaos.

Case Example: Alicia

Alicia, a 28-year-old single mom, was juggling rent, daycare, groceries, and car payments with barely anything left each month. One unexpected bill could knock her down for weeks. But after creating a simple plan — cutting a few expenses, adding a weekend tutoring side gig, and building a $500 emergency fund — everything shifted.

That small emergency fund changed Alicia's life. When her son got sick and she missed work, she didn't panic. She handled it. She felt capable. She felt steady. Stability didn't solve everything — but it gave her breathing room. And breathing room becomes decision room.

Milestone Moves for Stability

- Track where your money actually goes
- Pay bills on time (even minimums)
- Build a small emergency fund ($500–$1,000)
- Reduce unnecessary expenses without guilt
- Avoid new high-interest debt
- Celebrate every month that feels "less stressful"

Stability is the foundation of everything that comes next. Honor it.

Stage 2: Momentum (Building Speed and Confidence)

What Momentum Really Means

Momentum is where financial growth starts to feel real. This is the stage where you move from "catching up" to "moving forward." The energy changes. The mindset changes. The belief in yourself strengthens.

Momentum feels like:

- Progress
- Discipline that feels empowering, not restrictive
- Debt balances shrinking
- Savings growing
- Confidence rising
- A quiet fire inside you

Momentum isn't about perfection. It's about consistency. Step by step, month by month, you begin to see results.

Case Example: Bianca

Bianca, in her mid-30s, had been surviving for years. Once she reached Stability, she committed to eliminating her $15,000 of credit card debt. She sold her second car, took public transportation, and redirected every extra dollar toward her highest-interest card.

One by one, the balances hit zero. Each payoff gave her more confidence. Each win fueled the next. Within two years, Bianca was debt-free except for rent. She built a $5,000 emergency fund and began investing $200 a month in a Roth IRA.

Bianca didn't just gain financial momentum — she gained emotional freedom.

Milestone Moves for Momentum

- Choose one debt to eliminate and focus on it
- Automate savings and investments
- Negotiate interest rates and bills
- Increase income through raises or side gigs
- Build a 3–6 month emergency fund
- Track progress visually — charts, jars, or notes

Momentum is where you start to trust yourself again.

It's where identity shifts:

You stop feeling like you're drowning and start feeling like a woman who is rising.

Stage 3: Freedom (Work-Optional Finances)

What Freedom Really Means

Freedom is one of the most misunderstood milestones. It doesn't always look like retirement or wealth. Sometimes it looks like peace. Sometimes it looks like the ability to choose.

Freedom means:

- Your income is no longer survival-based
- You're not forced into toxic environments

- Your decisions come from intention, not desperation
- Your lifestyle is supported by what you've built
- You can say "no" without fear
- You can rest without guilt

Freedom is not a number — it's a feeling.

Case Example: Carmen

After 30 years of steady saving, paying off her mortgage, and building her retirement accounts, Carmen realized she could cover her essential expenses through investments and rental income. She didn't retire fully — she "pretired." She left her corporate job to consult on her own terms. She traveled more. She spent time with her grandbaby. She woke up with options.

Freedom isn't always loud. Sometimes it whispers, "You don't have to."

Milestone Moves for Freedom

- Protect what you've built through insurance and planning
- Set boundaries around your time
- Spend more in alignment with your values
- Explore passion projects
- Create a life rhythm that reflects what matters most to you

Freedom is living life by purpose, not pressure.

Stage 4: Legacy (Impact, Meaning, and Generosity)

What Legacy Really Means

Legacy is the stage where your wealth — both financial and emotional — overflows.

It's where your impact extends beyond your own needs and creates blessings for others. Legacy isn't about the amount of money you leave behind. It's about the love, wisdom, experiences, and opportunities you pass forward.

Legacy looks like:

- Funding scholarships
- Supporting ministries or nonprofits
- Helping children and grandchildren build stability
- Teaching financial values
- Creating generational patterns of wisdom and stewardship
- Building something that reflects your heart

Case Example: Denise

After selling her healthcare company, Denise reached a place of abundance. Her retirement was secured. Her children were stable. So she shifted her focus outward. She created scholarships for young women. She built a community park. She involved her children in her foundation, teaching them stewardship and generosity.

Legacy is where money becomes a message.

Milestone Moves for Legacy

- Write down your values and incorporate them into your financial plans
- Communicate openly with your family about your wishes
- Support causes close to your heart
- Work with advisors to protect and structure your giving
- Model generosity while you're still here, not only in your will

Legacy is long-lasting love expressed through financial wisdom.

Seeing Yourself in the Journey

Most women underestimate where they are. Some think they're in Survival when they're really in Stability. Some think they're in Momentum when they're stepping into Freedom.

Some are walking in Legacy without realizing the impact they already make.

This chapter is your mirror. Not to judge — but to show you your strength.

Ask yourself:

- "Which stage am I in right now?"
- "Which stage does my life feel like?"
- "What is one small step that honors this stage?"

Your answer doesn't need to impress anyone. It only needs to be honest.

Why Women Move Through Stages Differently

Women experience these milestones uniquely because so many factors shape our financial lives — caregiving roles, cultural expectations, workplace dynamics, emotional labor, and the pressure to put everyone else first.

Some women hit Momentum quickly but stall when life changes. Some reach Freedom at 55 because they paused their career for family. Some enter Legacy early because generosity is part of their identity. Some revisit Stability after divorce or illness, not because they failed, but because life shifted. There is no shame in moving between stages. It's normal. It's human. It's part of the journey.

The Emotional Shifts Between Stages

Your heart grows before your money does.

Stability → Momentum

Feels like waking up from fog. You begin trusting yourself again.

Momentum → Freedom

Feels like confidence. Like clarity. Like possibility.

Freedom → Legacy

Feels like purpose. Like your life is speaking louder than your words. These emotional transitions are milestones too.

Invisible Wins That Mark Your Growth

Real progress doesn't always show in your bank account.

It looks like:

- Checking your balance calmly
- Saying no to something that once tempted you
- Saving when you used to overspend
- Paying attention to your financial patterns
- Trusting yourself with decisions
- Choosing discipline over impulse

These invisible wins count. They build your identity as a financially grounded woman.

Charting Your Own Path

No matter your stage, honor it. You don't have to rush. You don't have to compare.

You don't have to apologize for starting where you are. Financial progress is a movement — not a moment. And you are already in motion.

Final Takeaway

Financial freedom isn't just a destination — it's a transformation. You honor your current stage. You build momentum step by step. You walk into freedom with clarity and confidence. You shape your legacy with intention and love. Your journey is sacred.

Your progress is real. And your next step is enough.

Chapter 13

The Feminine Future: Designing Wealth That Reflects Who You Are

What does it actually mean to live a wealthy life — not in the world's eyes, but in your own?

The truth is, there isn't one universal answer. And that's exactly why this matters. A feminine, grounded approach to wealth isn't about meeting someone else's standard of success. It's about creating a financial life that aligns with your values, your priorities, and the kind of woman you want to be.

Many of us start our financial journey chasing goals we never chose for ourselves — the salary we're "supposed" to earn, the house that looks impressive on paper, the lifestyle that signals we've "made it." And when we finally reach some of those milestones, we often discover they don't bring the satisfaction we expected. Instead, they bring pressure, stress, or the nagging sense that something still feels off.

In this chapter, we shift the focus inward.

This is where you define what enough means for you.

This is where you reconnect with your faith, your family, and your need for freedom.

This is where you design wealth that matches your values instead of someone else's expectations.

When your financial decisions reflect who you truly are, money becomes more than a number. It becomes a tool for building a life that feels authentic and balanced — not performative or exhausting.

Defining "Enough" and Success on Your Terms

One of the most freeing steps in your financial life is deciding what enough means for you.

Without that personal definition, it's easy to end up in a constant cycle of chasing "more": more income, more things, more status, more milestones. And if you're not careful, you can spend years achieving goals that never bring you peace.

Enough is not a specific dollar amount. Enough is a place where your financial decisions support your well-being, not drain it. Enough looks different for every woman. For some, it's financial security and a slower pace of life. For others, it's the freedom to travel, build a business, or provide opportunities for their children. The common thread is this: **your definition of enough reflects your own priorities, not the world's expectations.**

Take a moment to ask yourself:
What does success look like for me — honestly?

Maybe it's retiring at sixty with time for grandchildren.
Maybe it's traveling twice a year without stress.
Maybe it's a comfortable, paid-off home or the ability to give generously.
Maybe it's building a business that allows you to create jobs and mentorship opportunities for others.

None of these visions are wrong. What matters is that they are yours.

Real Talk: Success isn't one size fits all. It's defined by what supports your peace, not what impresses anyone else.

When you define both success and enough, you create a target that supports your life — not someone else's. It becomes a filter you can return to when you're tempted to compare, overextend, or chase a goal that doesn't actually fit your values.

Faith, Family, and Freedom: Your Wealth Priorities

To design wealth that truly reflects who you are, you need clarity on what matters most. For many women of faith, three pillars consistently shape their financial choices:

Faith. Family. Freedom.

These pillars don't replace practical planning — they guide it. They help you make decisions that reflect your values and keep your life aligned and grounded.

Faith

Faith shows up in your financial life when you allow your values to lead your decisions. This may look like:

- Giving regularly
- Supporting causes that reflect your beliefs
- Choosing investments or opportunities that align with your principles
- Trusting God's provision instead of living in constant anxiety

A faith-aligned financial life helps you hold money with an open hand — responsibly, but without fear.

Family

Family-centered wealth planning asks:

What decisions support the people I love and the relationships I want to protect?

This could mean:

- Choosing work that gives you time at home
- Saving for future opportunities for your children
- Preparing to support aging parents
- Creating experiences and memories instead of chasing material markers

Designing wealth around family helps ensure that your financial success strengthens your relationships instead of stretching them thin.

Freedom

Freedom is both practical and personal.

Practical freedom is the ability to make choices without being pushed by financial fear. No longer living paycheck to paycheck. No longer feeling trapped.

Personal freedom is the permission to build a life that reflects who you are — even if it doesn't match what others expect.

Freedom might look like:

- Paying off debt to create breathing room
- Building savings for flexibility
- Choosing meaningful work over high-pressure roles
- Creating time for rest, creativity, or community

Freedom allows you to shift from survival to intention.

Case Example: Sarah's Story

Sarah spent her early thirties climbing the corporate ladder in a demanding consulting firm. She earned well, but the cost was high — long hours, little connection with her husband, and almost no time for church or community.

After one particularly draining week, Sarah finally asked herself what she truly wanted her life to look like. The answer wasn't a title or a number. It was a peaceful home life. Time to volunteer. Enough income to live comfortably without burning out.

So, she and her husband made a thoughtful plan. They downsized their home, moved to a slower-paced town, and Sarah transitioned into a meaningful public-sector role that paid less but offered healthier balance.

Their income dropped, but their quality of life rose dramatically.

Sarah still saves for retirement, still plans, still stewards her money well — but she now measures success by alignment, not achievement. Her financial life reflects her values, not someone else's script.

Her story shows what happens when a woman trusts her own definition of a wealthy life.

Designing Your Feminine Financial Future

Designing your financial future starts with permission:

Permission to want what you want — and not want what you don't.

Not every woman wants early retirement.

Not every woman wants a high-powered career.

Not every woman wants minimalism, maximalism, entrepreneurship, or a traditional path.

Your financial plan should support your real life, not a life you feel pressured to adopt.

You might love your work and plan to continue for decades — but with more balance.

You might desire a simpler lifestyle to create margin for rest and family.

You might want to build something from scratch — a business, a mission, a legacy.

You might want seasons of intensity and seasons of ease.

The beauty of a feminine financial plan is that **it evolves with your life,** not against it.

It can help to write a simple vision statement — a paragraph that captures how you want money to support the life you are creating. It does not need to be perfect or poetic. It just needs to be honest.

Something like:

"I want my finances to give me stability, meaningful work, time with my family, and the freedom to give back. I want my money to support my values, not dictate my life."

Use your own words, your own priorities, your own truth.

Challenging Old Money Scripts

Many women were taught to stay quiet about money, accept whatever they're given, or put their financial needs last. These messages can follow you into adulthood unless you intentionally challenge them.

You are allowed to want financial stability.

You are allowed to make more money.

You are allowed to build wealth.

You are allowed to take up space in financial conversations.

You are allowed to protect your future and your peace.

Wanting financial strength is not greed. It is stewardship, self-respect, and wisdom.

A Future Built on Hope and Contentment

A healthy financial future holds two things at once:

- **Hope** for growth
- **Contentment** with your present

Hope keeps you moving forward. Contentment keeps you grounded while you get there.

When you combine the two, money stops being a source of pressure. Instead, it becomes a tool you manage with confidence and clarity.

Invite God into your planning. Ask for wisdom. Dream intentionally. And trust that you are being equipped for every financial season ahead.

Takeaway

True wealth is not measured by income or status.

It is measured by alignment — when your financial life reflects your values, your priorities, and your sense of purpose.

When your money supports who you are and what matters most, you're not just building financial stability. You're creating a life marked by authenticity, clarity, and peace.

That is the feminine future of wealth. And you have everything you need to design it.

Chapter 14

Legacy of Love – Planning for the Future

Estate planning might sound like something only wealthy people do, but really it's an act of love and care that anyone with a family (or even just possessions) should consider. It isn't just about money – it's about making things easier for your loved ones if something happens to you, and ensuring the values you hold can live on.

Think of estate planning as a powerful expression of **care and stewardship.** It's saying, *"I love my family enough to plan ahead so they're secure and know my wishes."* It might feel heavy to talk about, but there's real peace of mind in having these plans in place.

As one advisor notes, doing your estate planning is like writing a final love letter to those you leave behind – it spares them difficult decisions and chaos in an already hard time.

Planning for Your New Family

If you're a parent or planning to become one, estate planning is especially crucial. When I had my child, writing a will shot to the top of my to-do list. I wanted to legally designate who would care for my little one if I couldn't (that's what you do when you name a guardian in your will). It gave me immense peace of mind to know there was a plan, however unlikely the need.

For new parents (or grandparents raising kids, or anyone with dependents), getting these basics down means if life throws the unthinkable at you, your kids are protected. They'll have a guardian you chose, and access to funds you set aside, handled by someone you trust.

Extending Love to Home and Community

Legacy planning doesn't stop at your immediate family. It can reach beyond, to the community or causes you care about. Maybe you have a home that's been in the family – you can ensure it passes on smoothly. Or perhaps there's a charity, church, or scholarship fund you want to support after you're gone – you can include those wishes, too.

One woman I know set up her will to donate a small percentage of her estate to the community library that meant so much to her. It wasn't a fortune, but it was her way of extending her love of reading to future generations. That's legacy.

Estate Planning Essentials

Let's break down the must-haves for a simple yet solid estate plan:

- **Write a Will:** This is the foundation. In a will, you specify who gets your stuff (from money to personal mementos), and if you have minor children, you name their guardian. Without a will, state laws decide who gets what, which may not align with your wishes. A will can be done relatively inexpensively – even online templates or kits are better than nothing if you have a straightforward situation (though I recommend an attorney if you can swing it, especially with kids or significant assets).
- **Name Beneficiaries:** For many accounts like bank accounts, retirement accounts (401k, IRA), or life insurance, you can designate a beneficiary – the person who should receive the funds if you pass. Make sure you have up-to-date beneficiary forms on file for all these; those designations typically *override* what's in a will for those assets. So if you named an ex years ago on a 401k and never updated it –

yikes, they could legally get it. Review these annually or whenever you have a big life change (marriage, divorce, new baby).

- **Consider Life Insurance:** If anyone depends on your income (spouse, kids, aging parent), life insurance is a critical part of the plan. It provides a tax-free lump sum to your beneficiaries that can cover lost income, pay off a mortgage, fund college for the kids, etc. Term life insurance (coverage for a set number of years) is affordable for most people and often recommended over whole life for pure protection. A good rule of thumb is coverage that's ~10 times your annual income, but everyone's situation varies. The key is to think: if I'm not here, will those I care about be financially okay? If not, look into a policy.
- **Other Documents:** These aren't about death, but about being incapacitated. You should designate a **Power of Attorney** (someone to handle your finances if you can't) and a **Healthcare Proxy** or advance directive (someone to make medical decisions if you're unable). It's a tough thing to consider, but it spares your family a lot of anguish if something like an accident happens. Also, outline your healthcare wishes (do you want life support, etc.) clearly in those documents.

It sounds like a lot, but many lawyers do a bundle for a reasonable fee, or you can start with online services to draft these. The peace of mind is worth every penny and effort.

Saving for the Next Generation

Leaving a legacy often means investing in the next generation's future. If you have kids (or nieces/nephews/grandkids you adore), consider some tools to give them a head start:

- **529 Education Savings Plan:** These are tax-advantaged accounts specifically for education expenses. You contribute after-tax money, it grows tax-free, and withdrawals are tax-free if used for qualifying education costs (college, and even private school K-12 to some extent now). It's a great way to sock away money for your child's college and let it grow. Even small contributions over many years can add up thanks to compounding, easing the student debt burden later.

- **Custodial Accounts (UGMA/UTMA):** These are accounts you can set up for a minor where you contribute funds that become the child's property, but you (or whomever you designate) manage it until they reach adulthood (age 18 or 21, depending on state). The money can be used for anything benefiting the child – not just education. Do note the child will gain control at the age of majority, and it could affect college financial aid calculations somewhat. But it's a straightforward way to gift money/investments to a kid. Sometimes grandparents use these to gift stock or cash to a grandchild for future use.

Both 529s and custodial accounts are ways to put financial building blocks in place for those you love, while also teaching them about money as they grow (involve them when age-appropriate, show them how the account is growing, etc.). It's hands-on legacy building.

Values-Based Giving

Finally, think about aligning your money with your values even beyond your lifetime:

Your legacy can embody what matters most to you. Take time to reflect (and yes, even pray if that's part of your life) on the kind of impact you want to have. Maybe it's within your family, or maybe it's in your community or a broader cause.

- **Identify causes close to your heart:** Make a list of charities, communities, or efforts that mean a lot to you – whether it's your faith community, an alma mater, a shelter, a social justice cause, etc.
- **Use philanthropic vehicles:** If you're passionate about ongoing giving, look into tools like donor-advised funds (kind of like a charitable investment account), charitable trusts, or simply leaving a bequest in your will to a charity ("I leave $5,000 to X organization"). It doesn't have to be huge to matter – every bit counts to the organizations doing work you care about. And involving your family

in this (for example, telling your kids why you're leaving a portion to charity) passes on values of generosity.

By aligning your giving with your beliefs, you make a statement: that your life was about more than just your own needs, that you cared and acted on those cares.

Imagine the long-term joy of knowing your foresight is helping others or carrying forward a mission after you're gone. I think of it as planting seeds for trees whose shade I might not sit under, but future generations will.

Action Steps & Reflection

You can start strengthening your legacy right away. Two immediate actions to consider:

- **Name or update your beneficiaries:** Go through your retirement accounts, life insurance policies, etc., and make sure the right people (or charities) are listed. If you haven't named anyone, do it now; if you have old names (ex-spouse, deceased relative), update them. This is a quick task with huge implications.
- **Write a letter of intent (legacy letter):** This isn't a legal document, but it's heartfelt. Write a letter to your heirs or family, sharing any wishes or messages you want them to have. Some people use it to explain their choices (like why they left money to a certain cause), or to impart final life lessons and love. It's something your family can treasure, separate from the dry legal stuff.

By taking these steps, you transform abstract "plans" into concrete security and love notes for the future. You're basically saying, *"I care enough about what I've built – and the people I love – to guide what happens to it."*

That's a beautiful legacy in itself.

(We've covered so much ground! In the final section, let's bring it all together and send you off with encouragement and a vision for continuing this journey. You're almost at the finish line of the book – but the start of an amazing new chapter in life.)

Epilogue

The Journey Continues – Embracing the Feminine Finance Code

Reflecting on the Journey

Take a moment to look back at how far you've come. At the beginning of this journey, money might have been a source of uncertainty, fear, or even shame. Now, you've armed yourself with knowledge, strategies, and a fresh mindset. Before, you might have felt *alone* in your financial struggles; now, you know that countless others walk this path and that support and sisterhood are available to you. Before, the future felt daunting; now, it's lit by determination and hope.

There's a beautiful transformation happening. It happens slowly, in small shifts: the way you pause before a purchase, the way you speak kindly to yourself about money, the way you plan for tomorrow with faith instead of fear. These are not just financial shifts – they are deeply personal growth marks. **Celebrate them.**

Crafting Your Personal Finance C.O.D.E.

As you move forward, think about creating your own personal Finance C.O.D.E. – a set of guiding principles to keep you steady on this journey. Here's an example framework (feel free to adapt it or create your own):

- **Clarity:** Stay clear about where you are financially and where you want to go. Write down your goals – big and small. Continue to track your budget and net worth periodically so you always know the lay of the land. Clarity is power; when you know the truth of your situation, you can act on it.
- **Ownership:** Own every choice and every dollar. This is about responsibility and empowerment. No more blaming the economy, family expectations, or past mistakes – you and only you are in charge of your financial life now. That might sound heavy, but it's actually liberating. When you own it, you can change it. And remember, ownership also means owning your **worth** – never letting money (or lack of it) dictate how you value yourself.
- **Discipline:** Consistency is your secret weapon. It's not about being perfect; it's about that steady, continued effort. Keeping a budget, having those weekly money dates, saying no when a purchase doesn't serve your goals – those disciplined choices compound over time, just like interest. And on the days you slip (because we all do), discipline also means the grace to get back on track without punishing yourself.
- **Expansion:** Once you've stabilized your finances and built good habits, set your sights on growth and giving. This could mean increasing your investments, exploring new income streams, or leveling up your career – continually expanding what's possible. It also means expanding your impact: mentoring someone who's where you once were, or teaching your children and friends what you've learned, or contributing to causes you care about. A true legacy of wealth isn't just measured in dollars, but in lives touched and improved.

These four pillars – Clarity, Ownership, Discipline, Expansion – can guide every financial decision and reflect the balanced, holistic approach we've cultivated together.

Keep Learning and Growing

Peace is found in stability, but growth is found in movement. Don't confuse comfort with completion. You've come so far, and that progress deserves celebration — but don't stop there. Each new season of your life will call for a new level of wisdom. Keep stretching, keep learning, and keep trusting that your next financial chapter will expand what you've built with faith and perseverance.

The journey doesn't end here. In fact, it's just beginning. I encourage you to stay curious and keep educating yourself:

- **Books:** Continue reading books by and about women (and men) who have walked this road. For example, *"Clever Girl Finance"* by Bola Sokunbi is a great one, or *"Women & Money"* by Suze Orman, or any title that resonates with you. Every book might offer one new nugget or even just reinforcement of what you know – and that's worthwhile.
- **Podcasts & Blogs:** There's a whole world of personal finance content online that can fit into your life. Whether it's a podcast like *HerMoney,* a YouTuber who breaks down investing in plain language, or a blog about frugal living that gives you meal prep hacks – tap into those free resources to keep your motivation high.
- **Communities:** Plug into supportive groups. It could be an in-person investment club, a budgeting group on Facebook, a subreddit for personal finance, or just a group of friends who all want to improve their money game together. Surrounding yourself (physically or virtually) with people who are financially empowered creates a positive feedback loop. You'll feel less weird about your money goals when others are eagerly discussing theirs too!

Each resource and connection will keep your mind open and your confidence strong. And you'll inevitably pick up new tips as things in the financial world evolve (tax laws change, new apps come out, etc.). Staying engaged means you'll continue to make informed decisions.

Taking Action – Today and Tomorrow

Knowledge, as they say, is only potential power. It becomes real power when you use it. So let's talk about action:

What is one concrete step you can take *today* to cement your financial empowerment? Maybe it's transferring $20 into that emergency fund. Maybe it's increasing your 401k contribution by 1%. Maybe it's texting that friend to finally start the accountability partnership you talked about. Or writing in your journal about the money story you're leaving behind and the one you're stepping into.

Write a promise to your future self. It could be as simple as, *"I will check my accounts and journal about money every Saturday morning,"* or *"I will speak kindly to myself about money and not use the word 'broke' to describe myself,"* or *"I will seek guidance (from a mentor or professional) on investing by the end of this month."* Put that promise somewhere you can see it.

And don't forget to **celebrate your wins.** You have worked hard on this journey – honor that. Maybe you buy yourself a bouquet of flowers or a nice candle when you hit a milestone (paid off that credit card, hit $1,000 saved, etc.). Treating yourself in a planned, meaningful way reinforces that this is a joyous process, not a punishment.

Whatever actions you choose, do them **mindfully.** Each little step is a vote for the kind of life you want to create. They are evidence to yourself that "I am changing, I am growing."

A Final Blessing

I want to leave you with this affirmation – say it out loud, write it on a sticky note, make it your phone wallpaper, whatever keeps it in your heart:

"I am financially empowered, and this is just the beginning — we rise together."

Because you **are** empowered now. You've reclaimed your story, equipped yourself, and begun to walk in financial freedom. And this truly is just the beginning of what you can create when you combine knowledge with action, persistence with patience, and self-love with community support.

You are not alone on this path. You are part of a growing community of women who are taking control of their financial lives and cheering each other on. **We rise together,** lifting as we climb.

From the bottom of my heart, thank you for allowing me to share this journey with you. I'm incredibly proud of you. Keep that warm, empathetic, faith-grounded spirit as you go forth and conquer new heights. Your new money story starts now, with the very next choice you make.

With love and faith in you always,
Eva

Acknowledgements

To my family, who taught me that strength doesn't always roar; sometimes it prays, perseveres, and rebuilds quietly.

To every woman who has ever questioned her worth because of her wallet, this book was written for you. Thank you for reminding me that strength and softness can live side by side and that grace is a powerful teacher.

To my grandmother, my mother, every woman who mothered me, and every woman who made something out of almost nothing, your faith built the foundation for everything I stand on.

To my readers, for trusting me with your stories and your dreams. You remind me daily why this work matters.

And to God, my source, my anchor, my guide, thank You for every open door, every lesson disguised as a setback, and every ounce of grace that made this book possible.

Continue the Journey

Thank you for walking this path with me. If this book has touched, challenged, or inspired you, know that your journey doesn't end here — it's only beginning.

At MindExpand Publishing, we believe knowledge and faith grow stronger when shared. Visit our website to discover more books, free tools, and resources designed to support your next chapter of financial and personal growth.

Stay connected with me for upcoming workshops, new releases, and community updates — or simply to share your story. I'd love to hear from you.

Connect with Eva Deneux

Website: authorevadeneux.mindexpandpublishing.com

Email: evadeneux@mindexpandpublishing.com

Remember: Your financial journey is a lifelong act of courage, faith, and purpose. Keep learning, keep growing, and never stop building the life and legacy you were created for.

Reflection Pages

You've reached the end of The Feminine Finance Code, but your journey of growth and grace continues. These pages are your space to pause, process, and personalize what you've learned.

Take time to sit quietly, reflect on your progress, and remind yourself how far you've come.

Reflection Prompts

What have I learned about myself through my relationship with money?

How have I grown in the way I make, spend, and save money?

What does "financial peace" mean to me now — and what habits help me stay there?

What fears or beliefs am I finally ready to release?

How can I bring more openness and conversation into my relationship with money? Who can I talk to about my goals and challenges without fear or shame?

What legacy do I want my financial choices to build for my family, my community, and myself?

Affirmations for Your Journey

I honor my past and embrace my power to create a new story.

Money flows to me with purpose, peace, and integrity.

I make confident, faith-led financial decisions.

I am worthy of wealth, joy, and ease.

I give generously and receive gratefully.

I am rewriting my story — and this time, I am the author.

Take a deep breath. You've done the work. And this is just the beginning.

About the Author

Eva Deneux is a financial strategist, author, and advocate for women's economic empowerment. Drawing from her Sierra Leonean roots, U.S. Air Force discipline, and over 25 years in finance and operations, she brings a unique blend of practical wisdom and soulful guidance to the world of money management.

Her journey began with rebuilding from financial setbacks and transforming that experience into a mission to help others. Through *The Feminine Finance Code* and her publishing imprint, MindExpand Publishing, Eva shares stories that inspire growth, resilience, and self-worth across generations.

Her writing blends practical financial education with faith, empathy, and self-worth — guiding women to see money as both a tool and a teacher. She lives in Atlanta, Georgia, with her family and believes deeply that when handled with intention, money can become a sacred force for creating legacy and light.

Printed in Dunstable, United Kingdom

6378730e-bc2e-4e37-99d6-bc393cc8d012R01